Mark

Mark

A TWICE–TOLD TALE

WIPF & STOCK · Eugene, Oregon

Wipf and Stock Publishers
199 W 8th Ave, Suite 3
Eugene, OR 97401

Mark
A Twice-Told Tale
By Beaver, Caurie
Copyright©2004 by Beaver, Caurie
ISBN 13: 978-1-60899-121-1
Publication date 10/5/2009
Previously published by Xlibris Corporation, 2004

CONTENTS

CHAPTER I: FROM THE JESUS OF FACT
TO THE JESUS OF FICTION:
The Old Quest and the New 11

CHAPTER II: HEIRS OF THE VINEYARD:
Jesus' New Family 41

CHAPTER III: THE SCRIPTURES
AND THE POWER OF GOD:
The Scriptural Prophecies of the Passion
And Resurrection in Mark 65

CHAPTER IV: SPIRITUAL MEANING IN MARK:
All Things in Parables 97

CHAPTER V: SPIRITUAL BAPTISM IN MARK:
Dying and Rising 117

CHAPTER VI: SPIRITUAL FOOD IN MARK:
The Broken Bread and the
Broken Body of the Son of Man 137

CHAPTER VII: SILENCE IS GOLDEN:
The Motives of Jesus' Silencings in Mark 155

CHAPTER VIII: NARRATIVE WORLD
AND STORY WORLD:
The Two Beginnings And
Two Endings In Mark 169

CHAPTER IX: GOSPEL TRUTH OR
GOSPEL FICTION:
One Gospel Truth and Four Gospel Stories 183

CHAPTER X: TRUE ISRAEL:
Early "Christianity" As Messianic Judaism 199

APPENDIX
THE MESSIAH: God's Son Not David's 209

APPENDIX 2
THE GUIDING PRINCIPLE OF MARK'S GOSPEL:
Elijah Must Come First 217

AFTERWORD.. 243

ENDNOTES ………………………………….......... 247

To my wife, Sandra,
a gifted teacher and
my daughter, Kristen,
a poet in her own right.

"We ought at least to allow the complication that more than one wheel turns in biblical criticism. The Bible is the public book which is read and expounded in church. Since the Reformation it has also been a private book studied in studies. It is the book of God. It is also, as Herder read it, a human book. So two wheels turn, at least. One is public and theocratic, the other private and humanist."[1] —John Drury

CHAPTER I

FROM THE JESUS OF FACT TO THE JESUS OF FICTION:
The Old Quest and the New

The Pulpit and the Study: Practical and Theoretical Interpretations

Many Christians still believe that the scriptures can show them how to live in this world in order to be saved in the next; a few realize that the Bible also has a long history and contains specific references to the times in which it was written. Embracing the first view, preachers try to tell us what to believe about the scriptures, and scholars, following the second approach, attempt to teach us what to think about the Bible. The preacher is likely to tell us that there is only one way to interpret the scriptures—his way! He may also warn us that we cannot explain the Bible correctly without the Spirit (his theology) to guide us, that human understanding or reason, which is possessed by all, is not enough.

Instead of just one, the scholar is apt to present us with so many ways to interpret the Bible that he runs the risk of so confusing us that we do not know what to think. He sometimes claims that laymen are just not properly equipped to choose among the various conflicting opinions. Although the scholar may concede that the understanding required is a common possession of humanity, he reminds us that the proliferation of disciplines and methods has created a formidable barrier to the average educated person's gaining a genuine knowledge of the Bible. With this problem in mind John Drury wrote,

> The skills required are manifold and hard: knowledge of at least two ancient and two modern languages, of textual criticism and of testingly obscure episodes in history, of religion in its popular and its philosophical manifestations, of a vast and sometimes barely readable secondary literature."[2] Speaking to an audience at Drew University in 1974, James M. Robinson struck a similar note, "There is no such thing as the Prima donna who comes in as a brilliant amateur and sees what the stock-in-trade hack professor has not seen."[3]

To be fair, Robinson was calling attention to the undeniable fact that most books about the Bible written by amateurs were also amateurish. However, since Robinson uttered these words, things have changed considerably. With the application of literary critical methods to the Bible a number of "amateurs" have entered the field. Robinson, himself, has even written for just such a publication, *The Guide to Biblical Literature*, one of the editors and contributors of which, Frank Kermode, was an amateur in the biblical field at least.

It was to Robinson's credit that he recognized in principle the possibility of such contributions by amateurs and even welcomed them. At one time it was quite common, he said, for well educated non-theologians to write about the Bible. He called attention to the number of novels and non-scholarly books taken seriously by Albert Schweitzer in his *Quest of the Historical Jesus*. As a specific example of a work by such an amateur, Robinson held up the Jeffersonian Bible in which president Jefferson indulged in a bit of biblical criticism by cutting out the miracles in the New Testament because they offended his enlightened tastes. According to

Jefferson, morals not miracles proved the excellence of a religion; hence the title of the Jeffersonian Bible: The Life and Morals of Jesus of Nazareth.

Jefferson's contribution was made possible by the enlightenment philosophy which had created a widely shared vocabulary and set of concepts in terms of which such matters could be discussed. The subsequent age of professionalism tended to limit the discussion of religion to theologians and philosophers. Specialization gave rise to the extensive use of technical jargon that may as well have been a foreign language. Academic theologians combined an array of methods with the idealistic philosophy of the nineteenth century and the existentialist philosophy of the twentieth to form a manner of speech that to the intelligentsia was virtually an unknown tongue. In contrast literary critics have applied to the Bible a vocabulary and set of concepts that are comprehensible to theologians and intelligent laymen alike. Like the enlightenment philosophy, literary criticism has already created a climate favorable to the participation of educated non-theologians in biblical studies.

That which made it difficult for non-specialists to make a contribution to biblical interpretation was the sheer amount of material that one had to master in preparation for such a task. This circumstance separated biblical scholarship from other educational pursuits and created the impression that there was something qualitatively unique in its requirements. Obscured was the most basic prerequisite for biblical study, which was the same as for any other field of research, the sustained, disciplined application of human understanding, which has met with so much resistance in the study of religion. All week we use our common sense to collect facts, reject this story, accept that one, and make decisions of the most complex nature; then we go to church on Sunday and feel helpless when we are confronted with the same mixture of fact and fiction, of credible and incredible stories in the Bible.

The two approaches, the preacher's and the scholar's, correspond to two different ways of regarding the Bible, the practical and the theoretical. John Drury used two images to represent these divergent functions in biblical interpretation: the story of Ezra reading the Law from a pulpit, which was erected before the Water Gate, and Holbein's portrait of Erasmus working in his study. Due to the Mosaic ban on graven or visual images, the first is a verbal description found in the Old Testament book of Nehemiah, the second a painting. In response to the request of the people, Ezra brought the Book of the Law of Moses,

> "And he read from it facing the square before the Water Gate from early morning until midday, in the presence of the men and the women and those who could understand; and the ears of all the people were attentive to the book of the law. And Ezra the scribe stood on a wooden pulpit which they had made for the purpose;" (Neh. 8: 3-4a).

By reading and interpreting the Law, Ezra hoped to form a community of the Jews who had returned to Jerusalem from Babylon. Of the significance of this scene John Drury wrote,

> "The hermeneutical game had begun in a scene which corresponds very closely to the mise-en-scene of the Bible in English society two millennia later: the pulpit, the reading and exposition and the attentive congregation whose mind and manners are to be shaped by it."[4]

Like Ezra, our preacher still addresses the congregation from a pulpit urging them to live in accordance with the precepts of the Bible in order to create a community that is free of crime, drugs, and A.I.D.S.

If Ezra were a symbol of the practical application of the Bible to the problem of public order, Erasmus was a symbol of the theoretical study of the Bible, which ideally pursued the quest for historical truth without regard for consequences, not that it did not have any consequences. Pictures, however, can be very deceptive. On the surface Ezra, the preacher, appeared to have been in touch with many people, and Erasmus, the scholar, lonely and isolated. Just the reverse may very well be true. While the preacher speaks to hundreds, thousands, and even millions by T.V., it is a one-way communication: he speaks and they listen. In contrast the lone scholar in his study may be in genuine dialogue with hundreds and thousands of other scholars. Writing about the apparent isolation of the eighteenth century scholar, Anthony Collins, John Drury claimed that,

> "It was a seclusion which was always in touch with a wide and plural literary world: the "republic of letters" founded on the exchange of letters as well as the availability of books. As well as being the focus of a new intellectual richness it provided freedom to follow wherever truth might lead, unhampered by the immediate pressure of public order. The pluralism and the liberty sustained each other."[5]

The divergent concerns of the preacher and the scholar produced very different lives of Jesus: the preacher's practical interest produced a life of Jesus like Alfred Edersheim's *Life and Times of Jesus the Messiah*; the scholar's theoretical approach resulted in a study like Albert Schweitzer's *Quest of the Historical Jesus*. According to Edersheim,

> "We shall perceive that their form is wholly of the times, their cast Jewish—while by the side of this similarity of form there is not only essential

> difference but absolute contrariety of substance and spirit. Jesus spoke as truly a Jew to the Jews, but he spoke not as they—no, not as their highest and best teachers would have spoken. And this contrariety of spirit with manifest similarity of form is, to my mind, one of the strongest evidences of the claims of Christ, since it raises the all-important question, whence the teacher of Nazareth—or, shall we say, the humble child of the carpenter—home in a far-off little place of Galilee—had drawn his inspiration?"[6]

Edersheim described a Jesus, who was unique, superior to both his Jewish as well as his Greek environment. For Edersheim this uniqueness called into question the human origin of Jesus' teachings. They must instead have come from a divine source, he concluded, which gave them the authority required by the practical interest in compelling people to heed them and measure their conduct by them.

The elements of Edersheim's view have recently reappeared in a scholarly disguise. According to a current "scientific" method, a saying can only be considered a genuine saying of Jesus if it can be demonstrated that it was free of Jewish as well as Hellenistic influences. No doubt this view was the outcome of "scientific" rather than pastoral methods, but the results were similar: a unique Jesus who was separated from his Jewish and Hellenistic surroundings.[7]

Schweitzer's theoretical approach led him to portray a Jesus who was diametrically opposed to Edersheim's. Schweitzer's Jesus was a child of his age, influenced by the Jewish apocalyptic works, which are represented in the Bible by the books of Daniel and Revelation, but which also flourished in the intertestamental period. If Jesus predicted the imminent end of the world,[8] as Schweitzer thought, he was mistaken, a circumstance that reduced his authority from the absolute level required by the practical interest. In the practical view the Bible was the judge of one's thought and conduct; in the theoretical outlook one's own understanding was the standard against which the Bible was to be evaluated.

Even without the question of miracles, it was inevitable that the practical and theoretical views would clash. When the preacher looked at the Bible as a rule of faith and a code of conduct, he considered it a more or less unchanging standard; when the scholar viewed the Bible as history, he constantly revised his picture as new discoveries were made from the Dead Sea Scrolls to the Nag Hammadi Codices. The "shock" of such discoveries resulted from the intersection of the practical and the theoretical ways of regarding the Bible. The historian asserted that what the preacher said was the same yesterday, today, and tomorrow, changed!

Where do we stand today and why are practical concerns so prominent in our age? Although we have to an extent solved the political problem above the municipal level on the national scale, we still have international disorder. As the Hellenistic period was in transition from the city state to the "nation state," we are perhaps en route from the nation state to the "new world order." Like the Greek city states after the conquests of Alexander the Great, our own nation states are having difficulty defining their purposes in foreign affairs: Do they police the world or withdraw within their national boundaries and leave the world to its fate? In Hellenistic times a person was still a citizen of a city, and we are still citizens of nations not citizens of the world. The technological basis of a world order with world citizenship is rapidly developing. The obstacles to its accomplishment are largely cultural and historical. When the political problem is solved on the international level, one can expect theoretical interests to reassert themselves.

The preacher excluded every view of Mark that did not serve the practical aim of providing for salvation or public order. Radical accounts of Mark, such as Fernando Belo's *A Materialist Reading of the Gospel of Mark*, which were designed to subvert the present establishment, also belong here because they sought to replace the old order with a new one. In contrast scholars included as many views as possible; like the Parable of the Wheat and the Tares, they let the wheat and the weeds grow together until harvest. This inclusive tendency of scholars is well illustrated by Albert Schweitzer's *Quest of the Historical Jesus*, which grew out of the advice of that master of the theoretical interest, Aristotle! Concerning his histories of research on the Last Supper, the teachings of Paul, and the life of Jesus, Schweitzer wrote,

> "That I three times brought myself to follow such a laborious byroad is the fault of Aristotle. How often have I cursed the hour in which I first read the section of his Metaphysics in which he develops the problem of philosophy out of a criticism of previous philosophizing! Something which slumbered within me then awoke. Again and again since then have I experienced within me the urge to try to grasp the nature of a problem not only as it is in itself, but also by the way it unfolds itself in the course of history."[9]

With Mary Ann Tolbert's *Sowing the Gospel* literary criticism has come to encompass the entire Gospel of Mark. Earlier works treated Mark in a piece meal fashion using the gospel to illustrate the elements of literary critical method rather than to explain the gospel story.[10] Valuable non-literary critical contributions were made early on by Wrede, Lightfoot, Marxsen, and James M. Robinson. Other pieces of the puzzle will be found in John Drury's *Parables in the Gospels*, and M. Robert Mansfield's *Spirit and the Gospel in Mark*, which initiated the discussion of the Holy Spirit in Mark, a neglected subject. Finally, Quentin Quesnell in his *The Mind of Mark* attempted to read the mind of Mark and almost managed to do it. More than once we will draw from this very valuable work. Represented here are men and women, Catholics and Protestants, and even Marxists and Humanists.

Generally speaking the various elements of an interpretation of Mark are almost all present in the literature, but they are not found in a single work; they are scattered throughout the works of authors who are not yet in genuine dialogue with one another. It will be the present author's task to bring these observations together and to add important missing parts. As we consider Mark, let us imagine that the new world order is already here. As we look at what others have written about that gospel, we will ignore the walls that separate the various nations and different religious denominations. With Paul we will say,

> "There is neither Jew nor Greek, there is neither
> slave nor free, there is neither male nor female;"
> (Gal. 3: 28a).

We will judge a contribution not on the grounds of its origin, but on the basis of what it adds to our understanding of Mark. We will follow the advice of Aristotle and Schweitzer and begin with the history of research, the key to which is periodization.

Schweitzer and Robinson: Rightly Dividing the History of Research

The various methods by which New Testament theologians have studied Mark, and the different conceptions through which they have understood and explained that gospel are reflected in the divergent ways they have divided the history of research. The respective interests of the nineteenth and twentieth centuries are clearly revealed in the periodization schemes proposed by Albert Schweitzer and James M. Robinson for the history of research on the life of Jesus. Since Schweitzer's own studies concluded the life of Jesus movement of the eighteenth and nineteenth centuries, it was only fitting that he should have written its history in his *Quest of the Historical Jesus*. Wrede, whose book, *The Messianic Secret*, initiated the fictional view of Mark, could not have written such a history of research because the movement to which his work gave rise as yet had no history to narrate; to it belonged the future!

In the nineteenth century the focus was on the historical Jesus, not on the gospel of Mark. All comments about marcan authorship subserved the interest of proving that the gospel was a reliable historical source: its then recently discovered status as the earliest gospel, its supposed connection with Peter, and its apparent simplicity of style. This emerging historical interest was the dominant theme of the periodization scheme that Schweitzer suggested. He divided the history of research on the life of Jesus into three approximately equal periods each of which presented a choice between two alternatives. Regarding Johannes Weiss' *Preaching of Jesus Concerning the Kingdom of God* Schweitzer wrote,

> "He lays down the third great alternative which the study of the life of Jesus had to meet. The first was laid down by Strauss: either purely historical or purely supernatural. The second had been worked out by the Tübingen school and Holtzmann: either Synoptic or Johannine. Now came the third: either eschatological or non-eschatological."[11]

By the time James M. Robinson wrote his *New Quest of the Historical Jesus* it was clear that the view of William Wrede, which Schweitzer had designated as "thoroughgoing skepticism," had won the day. Although Robinson recognized the epochal significance of Schweitzer's achievement, the subsequent history of research compelled him to revise Schweitzer's periodization scheme. Robinson divided the history of research into two broad periods: the historical approach to Mark ended at the turn of the twentieth century to be followed by the rise of the theological, literary, or fictional view of Mark. Expressing the development in terms of a shift in the burden of proof, Robinson wrote,

> "In the nineteenth century the burden of proof lay upon the scholar who saw theological interpretations in historical sources; in the twentieth century the burden of proof lies upon the scholar who sees objective factual source material in the primitive church's book of common worship."[12]

Others have noticed the contrast between the nineteenth and twentieth centuries. Sean P. Kealy in his *Mark's Gospel: A History of its Interpretation* quoted Peter F. Ellis, who contrasted simple Mark prior to Wrede with not so simple Mark after Wrede,

> "The period of 'simple' Mark (Papias to Wrede) to the period of 'tricky' Mark (Wrede to Marxsen) on to 'subtle' Mark (Marxsen to Minette de Tillesse) and finally in recent years to 'theological' Mark."[13]

Frank J. Matera's *What Are They Saying About Mark?* also contrasted nineteenth century "historical" Mark with twentieth century "literary" Mark.

In his *A History of the Interpretation of the Acts of the Apostles* W. Ward Gasque objected to such periodization schemes as one-sided and simplistic.

> "An attempt to present a well-rounded, rather than one-sided, history of critical discussion has led me to regard the attempt to divide the history of research into neatly defined periods (e.g., the periods of *Tendenzkritik, Quellenkritik, Formgeschichte,* and

Redaktions-geschichte) as an oversimiplification which is more misleading than it is helpful."[14]

He also objected to the German domination of biblical interpretation, which is shown by the German terms by which the various methods and periods of research were called. However, Gasque's own bias in favor of the historical approach to Acts caused him to overlook the one method of biblical criticism contributed by English language theology and designated by an English term, Literary Criticism! The same bias led him to fail to mention even in his "Addendum: A Fruitful Field: Recent Study of the Acts of the Apostles," a very important study of Luke by a British scholar, John Drury, *Tradition and Design in Luke,* which contradicted Gasque's characterization of British scholarship as conservative.

Robinson's own *Problem of History in Mark* anticipated the redaction (editorial) and literary approaches in fashion today. The word "fiction" was not used by Wrede and Robinson to describe this new period since the turn of the century; the term "fiction" has only recently come into prominence with the application of literary critical methods to the gospels. However, in his history of research on the messianic secret James Blevins did use the word "fiction" to describe Wrede's view.[15] Randal Helm's *Gospel Fictions* was one of the few works that used the term "fiction" in the title of a book on the gospels, and Mary Ann Tolbert's *Sowing the Gospel* boldly discussed the gospel of Mark as fiction.[16]

By combining the periodization schemes of Schweitzer and Robinson, we arrive at the following outline of the history of research on the life of Jesus and the gospel of Mark.

I. MARK AS HISTORY: to 1900

A. Strauss: Philosophical Criticism.
B. H. J. Holtzmann: Literary (Source) Criticism.
C. J. Weiss and A. Schweitzer: Historical Criticism.

II. MARK AS FICTION: Since 1900

    A. Form Criticism: Mark as a collector.
    B. Redaction Criticism: Mark as an editor.
    C. Literary Criticism: Mark as an author.

The appearance of the term "literary criticism" in both periods requires an explanation. It meant something different to the historian than it did to the literary critic. The historian was primarily interested in events, and eyewitnesses, so he asked whether Mark was an eyewitness to the life of Jesus or included such accounts in his gospel. Nineteenth century scholars were preoccupied with the search for sources and understood that as literary criticism; it should have been and sometimes was called source criticism.

The literary critic was primarily interested in the structure of the gospel story rather than its sources. Not only was he not interested in the events, which Mark claimed to report, he may not even have been interested in the actual author and readers / hearers of the gospel. If he confined his attention to the text of Mark, then he could only have spoken about the implied or ideal author or readers / hearers suggested by the gospel.[17] As long as scholars considered Mark a historical report, they imagined that the author was someone who was close enough to the events to have witnessed them himself or to have obtained information from eyewitnesses. When Form Critics came to look upon Mark as a loose collection of stories, they described the gospel's "author" as a collector of anonymous communal traditions. When scholars began to regard Mark as a revision of an earlier oral or written tradition, they portrayed the gospel's "author" as an editor. It was only when literary critics recognized that Mark was a consciously composed artistic whole that they thought of the gospel's author as a creative writer. In all of this it is important to realize that nothing was known about the actual author of Mark. The type of author imagined for Mark was inferred from the description of the gospel that happened to be accepted at the time. In the language of literary criticism, scholars were not dealing with the actual author of Mark, but with the implied author.

While the historian concerned himself with something external to the gospel story, people and events, the literary critic studied the elements of the narrative, itself, characters and plots. The literary critic was interested in the gospel story for its own sake, not for what it could tell us about the history it claimed to relate. It has often been said that the literary critic did not treat the gospel story as a window on to history.[18] The gospel narrative was more like a stained glass window through which one got an occasional glimpse of the Jesus of history or the early church. The historian looked through the window at Jesus; the literary critic looked at the window, itself, as one might read the gospel story in the stained glass windows of some medieval cathedral. There is an initial and hopefully beneficial shock in thinking of Jesus as a character and his messiahship as a role in a story whatever they might have been in history. But first with Albert Schweitzer we will look through the window at the Jesus of history.

I. MARK AS HISTORY: to 1900

A. Strauss: Philosophical Criticism

That Schweitzer favored the historical approach to the gospels is evident from his formulation of the first alternative posed by Strauss: "either purely historical or purely supernatural." Nowhere did Strauss so state the matter. For him the "purely historical" was the rational interpretation, which he rejected along with the supernatural view in favor of the mythical explanation of the gospel stories. The supernatural view accepted the miracle stories at face value, the rationalist view looked in the stories for a misperception of a purely natural event, and the mythical interpretation sought to derive them from Old Testament prototypes or the communal consciousness of the early Christians.

That Schweitzer did not contrast the mythical with both the rational and supernatural views, as Strauss had, only showed how uncongenial the mythical explanation was for Schweitzer's basically historical approach to the gospels. His view was closer to the rational explanations of Reimarus and Paulus than it was to the mythical interpretation of Strauss. Like the rationalists Schweitzer accepted the gospel story as an eyewitness account, and sometimes attributed miracles to the misperception of ordinary events. The transfiguration was a vision like that of Paul on the road to Damascus.[19] The feeding of the multitude was a sacrament not a miraculous feeding of hungry people; one merely needed to strike out the assertion that the people were "filled."[20] For Schweitzer the significance of Strauss resided primarily in his uncompromising denial of the miraculous. Schweitzer did not follow Strauss when the latter extended the mythical explanation to the non-miraculous elements of the narrative. Once the troublesome question of miracles was disposed of, Schweitzer opted for the historical explanation of the narrative. Therefore, Robinson was right when he concluded that the mythical view of Strauss led directly to the skeptical view of Wrede, not to the historical view of Schweitzer.[21]

B. H. J. Holtzmann: Literary (Source) Criticism

The historical interest is also apparent from Schweitzer's second alternative: either Synoptic or Johannine, for he chose the Synoptic gospels over the gospel of John because he believed that the former were more reliable historical sources for the life of Jesus than the latter. Schweitzer's teacher, H. J. Holtzmann, had developed the Two Document Hypothesis to explain synoptic relationships. This theory accepted the priority of Mark and explained the other two gospels as the product of Mark and Q, the materials common to Matthew and Luke, but not found in Mark.

Both parts of the Two Document Hypothesis have been challenged recently: William Farmer denied the priority of Mark in favor of Matthew, and John Drury denied the necessity of the Q hypothesis.[22] James M. Robinson points out the main weakness of Farmer's argument: no redaction (editorial) critical study of Mark has been done based on the assumption of the priority of Matthew, which showed how Mark revised Matthew.[23] An unsuccessful attempt has recently been made by Harold Riley in his *The Making of Mark*. Riley argued that the account of the death of John the Baptist was clearer in Matthew where Jesus' withdrawal to the desert was motivated by his hearing of John's death (Matt. 14:13). Riley criticized Mark for not noticing this connection between the story of John's death and the next scene. Riley failed to notice that the death of the Baptist in Mark was a flashback (Mk. 6:14-29) for which Matthew, contrary to narrative logic provided a transition to the next scene.[24] This last point was made in an excellent study of "The Priority of Mark." by Styles.[25]

In contrast redaction (editorial) studies have been done for both Matthew and Luke based on the priority of Mark.[26] Therefore, it would appear that Mark was the earliest gospel. However, since Wrede and the redaction critics called attention to the dogmatic, theological, or fictional element in Matthew, Mark, and Luke, there is no longer such a gulf between them and the gospel of John; neither the Synoptic Gospels nor John's gospel is considered a reliable source for the life of Jesus.

The case for Q is not as strong as that for the priority of Mark. Of course, Robinson and others felt that the discovery of the Gospel of Thomas supported the Q hypothesis, but it did not prove it.[27] John Drury argued that there are other ways to account for the materials common to Matthew and Luke. He quoted James Hardy Ropes who wrote,

> "There is a simpler competing possibility, namely that Luke drew these sayings from the gospel of Matthew, which has never been shown to be impossible."[28]

In his studies of Luke and the parables Drury claimed that he was able to dispense with Q. His studies are so brilliant that one hesitates to dismiss his skepticism about the existence of Q. Besides, Q was the product of source criticism; literary criticism may eventually make the assumption of Q unnecessary. Although literary critics are not directly interested in source critical questions like that of Q, they may very well develop new ways of looking at the matter. Certainly, the recognition of the larger role of the gospel authors in the composition of their works will affect the way we view the sources that they selected and the way they arranged them.

C. Johannes Weiss and Albert Schweitzer: Historical Criticism

Finally, the historical interest shaped and dominated Schweitzer's third alternative: either eschatological or non-eschatological. Schweitzer thought that the eschatological explanation tended to support the historical reliability of Mark and parts of Matthew. He reasoned that no one would have attributed predictions of the end of the world to Jesus after the date that was set for the end had passed, a problem that he thought was posed by Matthew 10: 23!

> "When they persecute you in one town, flee to the next; for truly, I say to you, you will not have gone through all the towns of Israel before the Son of Man comes."

Of course, Schweitzer and others have assumed that this saying was a prediction of the end of the world. If so, it was unfulfilled, and who would have bothered to invent a saying for Jesus that had already been disconfirmed by the subsequent course of events. Since no one would have invented such a saying later, Schweitzer concluded that it was a genuine saying of Jesus. Even if he were correct in his assumption that we have to do with a forecast of the end of the world, Schweitzer would still have been obliged to explain how Matthew could have transmitted a saying that he could not have invented. This observation raises a substantial doubt that Matthew considered the saying a prediction of the end of the world, and the person who claims a meaning for the saying different from that given it by Matthew has the burden of proof. If the saying were not a prediction of the end of the world, then Schweitzer's argument for the historical reliability of the discourse in which it occurred would be weakened considerably. Again it is a choice between understanding the saying in the context of the ministry of Jesus or in the setting of Matthew's story of Jesus. Schweitzer chose the former; we will choose the latter.

II. MARK AS FICTION: Since 1900

A. Form Criticism: Mark as a Collector

When Schweitzer called attention to the simultaneous publication of his and Wrede's theories of the messianic secret, he was hinting at the independence of his discovery of the historical version of the theory. Wrede's skeptical version of the Messianic Secret Schweitzer traced to Bruno Bauer and others.[29] Although Schweitzer proudly called attention to Reimarus' anticipation of his own eschatological hypothesis, he appears to have been unaware that John Locke, two hundred years before, had published a historical version of the theory of the messianic secret in his

Reasonableness of Christianity. John Drury pointed to the undeniable parallels between the form of Locke's theory and that of Wrede. However, Schweitzer, like Locke, attributed the messianic secret to Jesus; Wrede attributed it to Mark.

The history of the West is characterized by a dynamism occasioned by the periodic "rediscovery" of forgotten epochs: the Renaissance's "rediscovery" of the Greeks, and the Reformation's return from church traditions to the Bible. To these we can now add Drury's "rediscovery" of the works of Deism.[30] What gave these early critics the courage to pursue a criticism of the Bible so penetrating that it is still of value today? The Deists could dispense with the Bible because they had natural theology. The Bible, they thought, could add nothing to our knowledge of God that could not be learned by a contemplation of his creation. Locke's confidence lay elsewhere. He could apply reason to the Bible because he believed in the essential reasonableness of Christianity as the title of his book showed. When Locke refined the tools of reason and applied them to the Bible, he was sure that reason would never be turned against Christianity. He reminds one of the leaders of the French Revolution who sharpened the blade of the guillotine certain that it would never be used on them. Both were wrong!

Speaking of forgotten epochs, why was the unitary view of Mark lost sight of after Wrede? The failure to immediately develop Wrede's theory was due primarily to the continuing influence of the historical approach to Mark. At the turn of the century the theory of the messianic secret assumed two forms: the historical view of Albert Schweitzer and the "fictional" version of Wrede.[31] The subsequent discussion almost always turned on whether the messianic secret was to be attributed to Jesus (Locke and Schweitzer) or to Mark and the early Christian community (Bauer and Wrede).[32] Rarely was the question raised as to whether the theory fit the facts of Mark; both sides assumed that it did.

The historical interest was also revealed in the fate of Karl L. Schmidt's theory of the geographical and temporal framework of Mark. Once Schmidt had shown that the framework was secondary, it was discarded as fictional; interest shifted to the little stories embedded in it. It was assumed that they contained an earlier, if not historical, tradition. Only later was this framework made the object of study by Loymeyer[33], R. H. Lightfoot[34], and Willi Marxsen.[35] C. H. Dodd argued anachronistically that the framework of Mark was historical. Recently, literary criticism has applied the techniques of narrative criticism to the fictional framework of Mark.

The complacency of Form Critics in accepting the results of Wrede and Schmidt as final only shows that their real interest lay elsewhere in the historical approach. As practiced by "conservatives" such as Jeremias and Taylor, the object of Form Criticism was the history of Jesus; as practiced by "liberals" like Dibelius and Bultmann, its object was the history of the synoptic tradition, or the early Christian community.

Because Form Critics directed their attention to the individual stories contained in the gospels instead of the framework or larger story, they minimized Mark's role as an author. They considered the gospel editors as collectors of anonymous communal traditions, which they strung together at random like pearls on a string, a metaphor that literary critics would later turn against them. Form Critics were under the spell of the notion of the early Christian community whose beliefs they found everywhere in the gospels. Form Criticism developed in an age that emphasized the importance of the community in the concept of the kingdom of God as it was developed in the German, British, and American Social Gospel. It was first necessary for this communal building to be built block by block before the rejected stone (Mark as a creative author) could take its rightful place as the cornerstone.

Although it was not their primary concern, Form Critics preserved the holistic view of Mark by their adoption of

Wrede's theory of the Messianic Secret. It was the overarching story that held the individual stories together the string on which the pearls of tradition were strung. Form Critics preserved and transmitted, but did not develop the theory. It was left for James M. Robinson to provide Wrede's view with an unassailable foundation by shifting the emphasis from the messianic secret to the parabolic secret. In this form the theory revealed its connections with a generally recognized type of Hellenistic literature which may be variously designated as parable or allegory.[36]

B. Redaction (Editorial) Criticism: Mark as an Editor

In our day the unitary or holistic approach to Mark has taken two forms: redaction or editorial criticism and literary criticism. English language theology was never comfortable with Form Criticism's analytical fragmentation of the gospel story. The German model for dealing with fictional narratives was the mythical interpretation of Strauss, which focused on the individual stories rather than the gospel story as a whole. The English model for dealing with fictional stories was the novel, which could accommodate the interpretation of large scale narratives such as the gospels.[37] This section will cover Redaction (Editorial) Criticism and the next literary criticism.

Because they accepted the results of Form Criticism, Redaction (Editorial) Critics considered their main task to be that of separating the traditions contained in the individual stories from their editorial framework (redaction). In his *Mark the Evangelist* Willi Marxsen called attention to the significance of the neglected fictional framework of Mark as an ordering agent in the narrative—the string on which the pearls of tradition were arranged. Utilizing the metaphor of pearls on a string, Morna Hooker, in a small but interesting book on Mark, made the "feminine" observation that pearls are not placed at random on a string, but rather are carefully selected and arranged according to size, color, etc.[38] Redaction (Editorial) critics paid attention to the way Mark arranged and interpreted these pearls of tradition. Of course, the task was easier in the case of Matthew and Luke because one of the works that they revised, Mark, was still available for inspection. Except for Old Testament quotations, the traditions used by Mark were not preserved apart from the gospel in which they were embedded. It was thought necessary to devise a method to separate the traditions from the editorial framework before a comparison of them could be made. Like poor Lazarus, the author of Mark was out of the tomb, but was still bound by the grave clothes of tradition.

Was Mark such a cautious editor that he changed only a few things here and there in the traditions to bring them into conformity with his own views? Or did he rather take his stand in his own communal faith and freely mold the past to meet the needs of his flock? Form Critics described a Mark who was almost completely subservient to traditions; Redaction (Editorial) critics pictured a Mark who cautiously changed the traditions here and there; finally literary critics portrayed a Mark who exercised a great deal of freedom in retelling the traditional stories. Mark's use of the Old Testament would suggest a high degree of creativity. The freedom exhibited by Mark's retelling of the story of Jesus was not unlike the creativity shown by the intertestamental writers' retelling of Old Testament stories—Jubilees, for example.

C. Literary Criticism: Mark as an Author

Although we have saved the discussion of it until the end, literary criticism was one of the earliest methods applied to the Bible in modern times—the first shall be last! Robert Lowth, an English bishop, published his study of parallelism in Hebrew poetry in 1753; it was entitled *De sacra poesi*

Hebraeorum. In this country what used to be understood as literary criticism of the Bible was the study of the English translation of the Bible. These literary critics did not work in the original languages of the Bible, but they did utilize the results of scholarly studies of the Bible. One such critic, Mary Ellen Chase, produced a study of almost the entire Bible entitled *The Bible and the Common Reader.* By today's standards the literary criticism involved was often simplistic and impressionistic, and frequently degenerated into an exercise in praise and blame.

While more recent literary critics utilized a more complex critical theory and worked in the original languages of the Bible, ironically, they often rejected past scholarly studies because of their supposed irrelevance to the literary critical project. Their works were informed by such sophisticated critical theories as Northrop Frye's *Anatomy of Criticism,* Wayne Booth's *Rhetoric of Fiction,* and Seymour Chatman's *Story and Discourse.* They even took into account ancient literary theory such as Aristotle's *Rhetoric and Poetics,*[39] and other ancient manuals of rhetoric in the hope of finding the literary critical theory that influenced the composition of the biblical books in the first place. Recent literary critics have also produced a literary study of the entire Bible called *The Literary Guide to the Bible* edited by Robert Alter and Frank Kermode, which contained the contributions of scholars as diverse as John Drury and James M. Robinson.

With the application of literary criticism to Mark the fictional framework has expanded into the fictional narrative. Literary critics have shifted the emphasis from Mark as an editor to Mark as a creative author. The traditions were still there with their supposed editorial modifications, but they no longer exercised a controlling influence on the composition of the gospel. The creator of Mark was recognized as an author in his own right—like Lazarus he was out of the grave clothes of tradition at last! In order to demonstrate that Mark was indeed a creative writer we are obliged to show that the individual stories in Mark become clearer when they are related to the general tendencies of the gospel; the over all themes of Mark should also become more intelligible in the process. In the words of John Drury, the little stories should get and give meaning in the context of the gospel story as a whole. Otherwise we would be compelled to fall back on some kind of fragmentation hypothesis.

Appealing to F.C. Baur's "tendency Criticism" of the last century, Drury chose to attack the partitioning of the gospel story where it appeared to have the greatest justification in the study of the parables. Drury called attention to the long standing practice of lifting the parables out of their gospel setting and interpreting them in isolation. However, the isolation was an illusion for without some kind of context interpretation is impossible. Closer observation revealed that, after the scholar took the parables out of the gospels, he transferred them to another context: the ministry of Jesus or the scholar's own philosophy or theology. Of the three principal contexts utilized, two were hypothetical: (1.) the life of Jesus had to be historically reconstructed before it could provide a setting for the parables; (2.) although the scholars theology or philosophy was immediately available, the parables' relationship to it was speculative; (3.) only the gospel narrative's setting was immediately given. No reconstruction was required in the case of the third context since that was the form in which the parables were received. Only in that setting were the parables likely to yield their secrets, and perhaps unlock the secret of the gospel of Mark as well.[40]

Quentin Quesnell also recognized the importance of context for interpreting specific passages in Mark. Through the prism of a single verse, Mark 6: 52, Quesnell analyzed spectroscopically the various layers of the gospel tradition. He placed the verse in four successive contexts and observed how its meaning changed: (1.) the immediate context, (2.)

the wider context, (3.) the gospel as a whole, (4.) and the early Christian thought world.[41]

Like Drury, Mary Ann Tolbert in her study of the parables called attention to three contexts; the gospel, the historical Jesus, and the scholar's philosophy. Of the three, she recognized that the gospel context was the only one that was given without reconstruction, and the one that limited the number of possible interpretations.[42] In her book on Mark, unlike Quesnell, who focused on a single verse, Tolbert concentrated on the gospel as a whole. By doing so she was able to determine the importance and bearing of the Parable of the Sower and the Parable of the Vineyard in the overall structure of the gospel of Mark. Mark had Jesus say of the Parable of the Sower, "Do you no understand this parable? How will you understand all parables?" (Mk. 4: 7). "This parable" stood for the individual story, and "all parables" the whole gospel. It was the author of the gospel of Mark who connected the part with the whole. Tolbert suggested that the interpreter who does not understand this parable will not understand the gospel as a whole.[43] Both Tolbert and Drury claimed that the Parable of the Vineyard recapitulated the gospel story as told by Mark. Drury said that the parable needed no interpretation since the gospel story, which was drawing to a close, interpreted it. The parallels between the Parable of the Vineyard and the gospel story should not only lead to an interpretation of the parable but also to a clarification of the structure of the Gospel of Mark.

The Preacher's Sermon and the Scholar's Text

The preacher's text differed from the scholar's in that it usually consisted of one or two short passages around which the minister built a sermon. Jonathan Edwards based his sermon, "Sinners in the Hands of angry God," on the text, "Their foot shall slide in due time." (Deut. 32:35 KJV).

Martin Luther, who was both a preacher and a scholar, built almost a whole theology upon a single text, "The just shall live by faith." (Hab. 2:4, and Rom. 1:17 KJV). Ideally a scholar's text referred to an entire book not just to a particular passage; the individual text of the preacher then drew its meaning from and contributed to the overall meaning of the work in which it was found.

After what Drury said about the remarkable tenacity of the sermon, it is understandable that the preacher's way of interpreting the Bible has penetrated to the scholar's study. Often even very good scholars selected a specific passage by which to interpret an entire work such as the gospel of Mark. We have already seen how Quentin Quesnell used the lens of a single verse, " . . . for they did not understand about the loaves . . ." (Mk. 6:52), to scan the text of Mark. James M. Robinson chose to understand Mark in terms of the saying about binding the strong man.

> "But no one can enter a strong man's house and plunder his goods, unless he first binds the strong man; then indeed he may plunder his house." (Mk. 3:27).

This passage revealed to Robinson the theme of the cosmic conflict between God and Satan that ran the full length of Mark's gospel.[44] St. Augustine quoted this same passage in connection with his discussion of the millennium and the binding of Satan in the book of Revelation.[45]

Without the help of such passages it is difficult to know where to begin or where to place the emphasis in our interpretation of a text the size of the gospel of Mark. As if to anticipate our dilemma, Mark had the habit of revealing his overall purpose through a series of strategically placed images that cast light on the story as a whole. The saying about binding the strong man was one. Another such figure, the present and absent bridegroom (Mk. 2:19-20), which encompassed almost the entire gospel, gave rise to an interesting interpretation of Mark based on the absence of Jesus after his death.[46] The "absence christology" contrasted with Matthew's "presence christology": "Lo, I am with you always, to the close of the age." (Matt. 28:20). More obscurely, perhaps, the parables had in view Mark's overall literary project (Mk. 4). We could add other such sayings that spoke more or less directly to the central purpose of Mark: the saying about the new patch on the old garment, or new wine in old bottles (Mk. 2:21-22), the one about the rejected stone that became the cornerstone (Mk. 12:10), and, finally, the saying about the smitten shepherd and scattered sheep (Mk. 14:27). However, before we use these passages to reveal the purpose of Mark, we should pay some attention to their relative breadth and interconnection. None of these images was as sweeping and clear as the parable of the Vineyard (Mk. 12: 1-11), which Drury felt that the whole gospel interpreted, and by which Tolbert interpreted almost the entire gospel of Mark.

"Whoever does the will of God is
my brother and sister and mother."
(Mk. 3:35)

CHAPTER II

HEIRS OF THE VINEYARD:
Jesus' New Family

Jesus' Relatives In Mark

Inadequate information makes the historical problem of Jesus' family a very difficult one to solve; the same is not true of the literary portrayal of Jesus' family in Mark. Because of the self-referencing nature of the story, virtually all the information required to solve the problem is contained in Mark's gospel. Mark probably wrote for a Jewish and gentile community that claimed to be the heir of Jesus who was Jewish. Since the gentiles could not claim to be Jesus' relatives, they rejected natural kinship as the basis of their community. Following a gentile convention that deified exceptional persons, the Markan community already considered Jesus divine. Mark merely specified that Jesus was God's beloved son and heir, and redefined the family of Jesus as the ones who did the will of God. Both Jews and gentiles could then become relative and heirs of Jesus.

With the possible exception of the biography of God, who presumably had no parents, the story of a person's life almost always begins with or later flashes back to his or her family. The chain of begets in Genesis linked the persons named to a particular people, which immediately gave them an ethnic, cultural, and religious identity. In our day the story of Roots revolved around the loss of African identity in American slavery and its dramatic recovery. In ancient times perhaps more than now one's family defined one's character and limited his or her prospects. When meeting a stranger, the inevitable question was, "Whose son (or daughter) are you?" Even Jesus did not escape this ordeal of identification, for it may be argued that the central question of the gospel of Mark was not whether Jesus was the Messiah, but rather, as the Messiah, whose son was he? Was he the son of David or the son of God (Mk. 12:35-37)? The answer was given in the very first line of the gospel.

> "The beginning of the gospel of Jesus Christ, the Son of God;" (Mk. 1:1)

The division of labor between the theologian and historian has until now concealed a problem in regard to the family of Jesus: the theologian dealt with Jesus' heavenly connections, and the historian with his earthly family. No such neat division is found in the gospels, in which God through the Holy Spirit conceived the earthly Jesus, and Mary gave birth to the son of God. In contrast to the theologian and historian the literary critic must deal with the family of Jesus as it is portrayed in the gospels, which included his divine as well as his human relatives. Among the gospels Mark's treatment or mistreatment of Jesus' earthly family is unique: at one point his family went to seize Jesus because they thought he was insane (Mk. 3:21). When they arrived, Jesus refused to recognize them as his family. Pointing to the ones who sat around him, he said,

> "For whosoever shall do the will of God, the same is my brother, and my sister, and mother." (Mk. 3:35).

Mark's emphasis on Jesus' divine family is clear at the outset, for he began not with Jesus' earthly family, but his heavenly one. After introducing Jesus as the son of God, Mark's gospel failed even to mention his earthly father. Mark's bias in favor of Jesus' divine lineage explains his negative attitude toward Jesus' mother and brothers, whom he named, and his sisters, whom he did not name. Because he did not view Jesus' divine sonship in biological terms, the relationship between God and Mary was not a problem for Mark as it was for Matthew and Luke. Mark simply had God call Jesus' sonship into existence by a voice from heaven (Mk. 1:11), as he had created the world in the beginning with his word. Previously, the household of God had only servants, Moses and the prophets, but not children. Henceforth, God's expanding family will include his beloved son whose brothers, sisters, and mother are the ones who do God's will. It will include Jesus' earthly family only if they do the will of God.

From the fact that a number of Hellenistic and Roman rulers were paid divine honors we may infer that in Hellenistic culture a person born of human parents could and did acquire divine status. It is only the more primitive notion that traced the rulers' lineage back to divine parents. Whereas in a Hellenistic context such popular notions were tolerated, in a Jewish setting, at least where Hellenistic culture was not in complete ascendancy, such ideas would have been a cause for considerable concern. Luke combined the two options: Not only was Jesus directly conceived by the Holy Spirit, but his genealogy also ended with God.

> "... which was the son of Seth,
> which was the son of Adam,
> which was the son of God." (Lk. 3:38).

When Luke had the Holy Spirit come upon Mary, the power of the Highest overshadow, and impregnate her (Lk. 1:35), he brought back at one stroke elements that were long resisted by Jewish monotheism—sex between God and humans and generation and multiplicity within God. Matthew was equally explicit, "... for the child conceived in her is from the Holy Spirit." (Matt. 1:20; See also 1:18).

All that was lacking was the divine DNA. Christianity has since attempted to rid itself of the contradiction between monotheism and the resulting polytheism by means of the frozen theogony of the trinity. Although he had a son, God would nave no grandchildren!

The birth stories explained how Jesus was the son of God; Matthew with the genealogy also wished to claim that he was the son of David. David was even mentioned before the more remote ancestor of the Jewish people, Abraham.

> "The book of the lineage of Jesus Christ, the son of David, the son of Abraham." (Matt. 1:1).

In the summary of the genealogy David was mentioned twice (Matt. 1:17), and, finally, Joseph was called the son of David (Matt. 1:20). It has long been recognized that there was no need to present Joseph's genealogy unless he was Jesus' father. If Jesus were conceived by the Holy Spirit before Joseph had marital relations with Mary, then Joseph was Jesus' step-father. While Joseph's genealogy might prove that he was the son of David, it could not prove that Jesus was. Matthew deftly sidestepped this problem by calling Joseph not the father of Jesus but " . . . the husband of Mary, of whom Jesus was born . . ." (Matt. 1:16). Compare Luke's similar awkward handling of precisely the same problem: "He was the son (as was supposed) of Joseph . . ." (Lk. 3:23).

Mark did not include a genealogy because he argued that Jesus, as the son of God, was David's Lord and not his son (Mk. 12: 35-37). If Jesus had been the son of David, then he and his followers would have been tenants of God's vineyard like the Jewish leaders. Since Jesus was the Son of God, his followers were the heirs, not the tenants of God's vineyard.

Jesus' designation as the Son of God was crucial for the inheritance argument that Mark utilized in the Parable of the Vineyard. The inheritance metaphor, which was widely used in early Christianity (Gal.4:21-31; Heb. 3:1-6), was fundamental to the Markan community's consciousness of its right to exist. We can only touch briefly on the broader employment of the inheritance argument in the establishment of Christianity. Jeffrey Siker's *Disinheriting the Jews*[47] contains an excellent discussion of this subject in connection with the Abraham traditions. The Christians were so successful in claiming to be the true heirs of the Jewish tradition that the ancient history of the Christian Roman Empire became, instead of the early history of the City of Rome, the Old Testament history of Israel!

Because of the remarkable correspondence between the Parable of the Vineyard and Mark's story of Jesus, it is surprising how few scholars have used the parable to reveal the meaning of Mark. John Drury recognized that the Parable could only be interpreted in the setting of the gospel story as a whole, but his primary focus was on the Parables in the Gospels (the title of his book)[48] rather than on the gospels containing the parables. By interpreting the parables in the context of the gospels, instead of in isolation, his work at one stroke made obsolete almost the whole history of parable interpretation from Jülicher to Jeremias. In her book *Sowing the Gospel*[49] in chapters entitled "Jesus the Heir of the Vineyard" and "The Death of the Heir" Mary Ann Tolbert utilized the Parable of the Vineyard to interpret the gospel of Mark.

Mark's version of the Parable reads as follow:

1. "A man planted a vineyard, and set a hedge around it, and dug a pit for the wine press, and built a tower, and let it out to tenants, and went into another country.
2. When the time came, he sent a servant to the tenants, to get from them some of the fruit of the vineyard.
3. And they took him and beat him, and sent him away empty handed.

4. Again he sent to them another servant, and they wounded him in the head, and treated him shamefully.
5. And he sent another, and him they killed; and so many others, some they beat and some they killed.
6. He had still one other, a beloved son; finally he sent him to them, saying, 'They will respect my son.'
7. But those tenants said to one another, 'This is the heir; come, let us kill him, and the inheritance will be ours.
8. And they took him and killed him, and cast him out of the vineyard.
9. What will the owner of the vineyard do? He will come and destroy the tenants, and give the vineyard to others" (Mk. 12:1-9, R.S.V.).

In the Parable (God) the owner of the vineyard (Israel) sent his servants (prophets) to collect the rent from the tenants (the Jewish leaders). Finally (at the End of the World), the owner sent his beloved son (Jesus), and the tenants killed him so they could claim ownership of the vineyard. Mark said that God would destroy the tenants and give the vineyard to others, his community.

When the tenants killed the beloved son, "they ... cast (Εξέβαλον) him out of the vineyard," which may anticipate the transfer of the vineyard to Mark's community. The same Greek word was used in the Syro-Phoenician woman's story where Jesus said, " ... for it is not right to take the children's (Israel's) bread and throw (βάλειν) it to the dogs (gentiles)." (Mk. 7:27). The connection becomes even clearer when we realize that the crumbs that the Syro-Phoenician woman said that the dogs (gentiles) could eat (Mk. 7:28) represented the broken body of the Son of Man. Mistaking the vineyard for Jerusalem instead of Israel, Matthew and Luke attempted to correct Mark's story. They put the casting out of the vineyard before the killing of the son to make the Parable consistent with the story of Jesus' death outside Jerusalem (Matt. 21:39, and Lk. 20:15).

Because the Jewish leaders understood that Jesus had told the Parable against them, they tried to arrest him. In other words they were about to do to Jesus what the tenants in the Parable did to the son. Only fear of the people prevented them from carrying out their plan (Mk. 12:12), as it had earlier when Jesus "cleansed" the Temple (Mk. 11:18).

If the Parable of the Vineyard simply repeated the gospel story, it could tell us no more than the gospel told us. But it did more than repeat; it interpreted. According to Drury the parable

> " . . . is more overtly symbolic, which relates its own masked characters and events indissolubly to the real characters and events of the larger historical tale which it explicates."[50]

Like all sects, Mark's community laid claim to a legitimate succession of prophets in order to establish itself. At this point in the Parable the reader expects Jesus to be the latest in a long line of servant prophets, but this was not to be the case. Not only were the Jewish leaders downgraded by being called tenants of the vineyard instead of owners, but also the prophets were "demoted" to servants in comparison with Jesus, the beloved son and heir. There is a very close parallel in the book of Hebrews where Moses was called a servant in the house of God and Jesus a son and heir of all things (Heb. 3:5-6).

If Jesus were the son, he clearly inherited the vineyard, but it is not clear how God's giving the vineyard to the gentiles also made them heirs. To have been heirs the gentiles would have to have been Jesus' relatives, a fact not lost on Mark.

That is the point of Mark's mention of Jesus' relatives twice: once when Jesus' mother and brothers came to get him, and again when Jesus visited his home town. Mark intended these two scenes to be compared because he mentioned the same relatives in both instances: mother, brothers and sisters. Mark did not mention Jesus' father probably because he considered God his father. Matthew made good Mark's omission when he wrote, "Whoever does the will of my father in heaven is my brother, and sister and mother." (Matt. 12:50) In the first scene Jesus said, "Whoever does the will of God is my brother, and sister, and mother." (Mk. 3:35) This was an implicit rejection of his natural mother and brothers, who had come for him, unless they did the will of God. The counterpart to this story was the report of Jesus' rejection by the people of his home town, who showed that they did not understand the basis of kinship to Jesus because they pointed to his natural relatives instead of to the ones who did the will of God. The townspeople said, "Is not this the carpenter, the son of Mary and brother of James and Joses and Judas and Simon, and are not his sisters here with us?" (Mk. 6:3). Matthew made Jesus the carpenter's son (Matt. 13:55).

On another occasion when Jesus' disciples protested that they had left everything to follow him, he reminded them that they would be compensated. If they had left house, brothers, sisters, mother, father, children, and lands, they would " . . . receive a hundred fold now in this time, houses and brothers and sisters and mothers and children and lands with persecutions, and in the age to come eternal life." (Mk. 10:28-30). All these new relatives came from the ones who did the will of God. In the second list only the father was not mentioned, perhaps because in the Markan community God was their father. This is the counterpart to Mark's failure to mention Jesus' father in the earlier stories about Jesus' relative (Mk. 3:32 and 6:3).

The Parable of the Vineyard may also enable us to ascertain the relative significance of the various messianic titles in Mark: Christ, Messiah, Son of God, Son of Man, and Son of David. In the first half of Mark the question was, "Who was Jesus?" After Jesus stilled the storm, his disciples asked, "Who then is this that even wind and sea obey him?" (Mk. 4:41). At Jesus' baptism God said, "Thou art my beloved son . . ." (Mk. 1:11) and at the Transfiguration God said "This is my beloved Son . . ." (Mk. 9:7). "Beloved Son" was a designation that also appeared in the Parable of the Vineyard (Mk. 12:6). As part of the supernatural realm, demons also recognized that Jesus was the Son of God (Mk. 1:24 and 5:7).

In contrast to God and the demons, human beings in the first half of Mark thought that Jesus was simply a man. Herod said that he was John the Baptist risen from the dead; others thought that Jesus was Elijah or a prophet (Mk. 6:14-16 and 8:28). When Jesus asked his disciples who they thought he was, Peter said, "You are the Christ." (Mk. 8:29).

Once it was known that Jesus was the Christ, the question for the second half of Mark became, Whose son was the Christ? (Mk. 12:35) Peter knew that Jesus was the Christ, but did not yet understand that Christ was the Son of God. For the disciples the teaching about Jesus' divine sonship began at the Transfiguration just after Peter's messianic confession; they had not heard God's voice at Jesus' baptism because Jesus called them after his baptism by John. Although Jesus' identity as the Son of God was known to the reader (Mk. 1:10), to God (Mk. 1:11, 9:7), and to the demons (Mk. 1:24 and 5:7), the first human to recognize it was the Centurion at the cross. He said, "Truly this was the Son of God." (Mk. 15:39). However, it was in the Parable of the Vineyard that we learned why this title was so important to Mark: it was required by the inheritance argument. It was not just as a prophet or even as a son, but as the beloved Son that Jesus inherited the Vineyard. At his trial Jesus' answer to the High Priest presupposed the equivalence of the titles Son of God and Son of Man (Mk. 14:61-62).

Now it is clear why Mark had Jesus deny that Christ was the son of David; Jesus asked,

> "How can the scribes say that the Christ is the son of David?" David himself, inspired by the Holy Spirit declared, 'The Lord said to my Lord, Sit at my right hand, till I put thy enemies under thy feet.' David himself calls him Lord; so how is he his son?'" (Mk. 12:35-37).

When Jesus asked, "How can the scribes say that the Christ is the son of David?" he was referring to the traditional belief that the Messiah would be a deliverer from the royal house of David. In New Testament times there were a number of sectarian alternatives to this scribal expectation. The Qumran Community may have expected a priestly Messiah; the Markan community also called into question the scribes' exclusive claim for a royal Davidic descent for the Messiah, and supported its view with "inspired" scriptural interpretation.

If Christ had been the son of David, the Jewish leaders' claim to be the true heirs of the vineyard would have been valid. Mark had to insist that the Christ was not David's son, but David's Lord and God's son, so the gentile Christians could inherit the vineyard through him. If the Messiah were David's Lord, then David would have been a servant like the prophets in the parable. The scribes, who called Christ the son of David, were the ones against whom Jesus had spoken the Parable. When Jesus entered Jerusalem, the crowd did not call him the son of David, but only referred to the kingdom of David. They shouted, "Blessed is the kingdom of our father David that is coming." (Mk. 11:10). The kingdom of our father David stood in contrast to the kingdom of God that Jesus announced earlier (Mk. 1:15). Only Matthew had the crowd shout, "Hosanna to the son of David!" (Matt. 21:9). There was also a contrast between the crowd's father, David, and Jesus' father, God!

One story in Mark appears to have affirmed the Davidic sonship of Jesus. Bartimaeus at Jericho called Jesus the son of David, but he was blind, and blindness in Mark stood for slowness of wit or lack of understanding (Mk. 10:46-52). Donald Juel suggested that Bartimaeus' "confession" of Jesus as the son of David showed that, " . . . the blind man sees what Jesus' disciples (and the authorities) cannot."[51] However, special insight was not attributed to the other blind man in Mark, who saw men like trees walking before Jesus healed him completely (Mk. 8:24). Moreover, it was only after Bartimaeus was cured of his blindness that he "followed him (Jesus) on the way" (of suffering), and no longer called Jesus the son of David.

The Parable of the Vineyard may also enable us to rule out another title often claimed for Jesus, the Suffering Servant. Although the title did not appear in Mark, some scholars believe that it was the basis of that gospel's portrayal of Jesus' sufferings. The Parable described the prophets not Jesus as suffering servants; Jesus was the suffering beloved son.

Mark's inheritance argument established the community by laying claim to a succession of true prophets. After all, the servants were also sent by God, the owner of the vineyard. However, the appearance of the son marked a radical departure: his coming was introduced by the word "finally" (εσχατον), as the beloved son, he was the heir not just a servant prophet, and his death effected a transfer of the vineyard from the Jewish leaders to the Markan leaders.

Sometimes a figure of speech like the inheritance metaphor implies more than it says. After all, inheritance normally requires the death of someone. The gentiles inherited the vineyard when Jesus died, but how did Jesus inherit the vineyard before God died? In the 1960's certain theologians maintained that God did die or was killed by secularism, but that is a modern phenomenon unknown in ancient times. In the inconsistent thinking of Greek myth the gods were immortal, but could age. Likewise, in the Bible God did not die, but he did age; Daniel described him as the ancient of days. Jack Miles' biography of God is an excellent but not a definitive biography.[52]

If God did not quite die in Hellenistic and Roman times, he did become more distant. From a tribal God of the Jews he became the most high God of heaven and earth. His responsibilities were so broad that it became necessary for him to operate through intermediaries such as the Logos the Spirit, or Jesus, himself. Like some Hellenistic ruler or Roman Emperor he became so remote that he had to delegate to underlings the interaction with his many subjects. Rarely did God speak directly in the gospel of Mark, at Jesus' baptism (Mk. 1) and transfiguration (Mk. 9:), and there only to commend his intermediary the beloved son, Jesus. Even now Jesus is the operative God of many Christians. They accept Jesus as their personal Savior, and in prayer they ask Jesus into their hearts, not God!

The Death of Jesus' Auditors

When the tenants of the vineyard killed the beloved son, Jesus asked, "What will the owner of the vineyard do?" Answering his own question he continued, "He will come and destroy the tenants, and give the vineyard to others." By portraying God as an angry father who avenged the murder of his son, Mark drew a causal connection between the events that were separated by at least three decades: the death of Jesus, which occurred in the thirties C.E., and the destruction of Jerusalem (the tenants), which happened in the sixties C.E. How can we reconcile the apparent contradiction between the parable in which the tenants were destroyed without delay and the actual history in which Jerusalem and the Jewish leadership were destroyed only after some thirty years had passed? Or perhaps we should ask how Mark bound together these widely separated events. It may be helpful to use an analogy from secular history. We know from Josephus' account that the issues that led to the war between Rome and Judea were festering since the first part of the century when Judea became a Roman province governed by a Roman official. We are unaware of a gap here because the underlying conditions that led to the conflict continued to operate throughout the intervening decades.

The same may have been true for Mark with religious issues replacing political ones. Elaine Pagels described the gospel as "wartime literature."[53] Mark's primary focus was the war and its consequences: The downfall of the Jewish leadership and the suffering of the Markan community. He brought in the story of Jesus to explain what was happening in his own day. According to Mark the Jewish leadership was collapsing because of what Herod did to John the Baptist, and what the chief priests, scribes and elders did to Jesus, and continued to do to Jesus' followers. For Mark's community this was good news (gospel), because it meant that the vineyard, the Kingdom of God, was given to them.

By exonerating Pilate, Mark placed the responsibility for Jesus' death squarely on the chief priests, scribes, and elders. The parable had said "He (God) will come and destroy the tenants . . .," but the Romans came instead, apparently as God's instrument, and destroyed Jerusalem and the Jewish leadership. The parable had also said that God " . . . will give the vineyard to others." Of course, Mark understood these "others" as his community, but his claim did not go unchallenged. Having broken the power of the Sadducean priesthood, the Romans facilitated the rise of the Pharisees, which brought them into conflict with Jesus' followers. Whereas in Mark Jesus enemies were the chief priests, scribes and elders, in Matthew his principal opponents were the Pharisees. The break between the Jewish and Markan community, which included a considerable Jewish element, was hastened by two events that happened to coincide: the destruction of Jerusalem and the death of Jesus' auditors, most of whom were Jewish. Since the destruction of Jerusalem by the Romans was a newsworthy event, the Jewish general turned journalist, Josephus, wrote about it extensively. In contrast the death of Jesus' auditors was an occurrence of interest to only a few, so documentation for it was sparse. Probably neither Paul nor Mark was an eyewitness to Jesus, himself, but both were likely witnesses to the generation that heard Jesus speak. There was of course, a language barrier: Jesus presumably spoke Aramaic and Mark wrote in Greek, but Paul spoke Aramaic and wrote in Greek. From his correspondence we know that Paul was in touch with Jesus' followers, and Mark may have known of survivors from Jesus' day, so what they have to say about Jesus' auditors could prove to be of some value.

However, just when we are ready to listen to Paul, he disappoints our expectations and preferences for eyewitness reports by deliberately rejecting them in favor of divine revelation. Paul prided himself on his independence from the original followers of Jesus. After his "conversion," Paul said that he did not go up to Jerusalem immediately, but instead spent fourteen years in Arabia (Gal. 1:17). He disclaimed an interest in the Christ "after the flesh" (II Cor. 5:16). It was only when he spoke about the Christ after the Spirit, the risen Christ, that he had recourse to a tradition that was delivered to him (I Cor. 15:1-8). Included in his list of witnesses to the resurrection (sic.)—among whom he counted himself—were 500 brethren.

> "Then he appeared to more than five hundred brethren at one time, *most* of whom are still alive, though *some* have fallen asleep." (I Cor. 15:6; compare I Thess. 4:13-14).

This does not tell us much about the "auditors" of Jesus, but compensates by its probable accuracy. It is likely that *most* of the auditors of Jesus were still alive when Paul wrote. It is also likely that *some* had died.

MARK

By the time Mark wrote his gospel in the sixties C.E. we would expect these proportions of survivors to deceased to be reversed and that is precisely what we find.

> "And he (Jesus) said to them, 'Truly, I say to you, there are *some* standing here who will not taste of death before they see that the kingdom of God has come with power.'" (Mk. 9:1).

When Paul wrote, *most* of the witnesses to the risen Jesus (sic) were still alive, but *some* were dead.[54] By the time Mark wrote *most* of Jesus' auditors were dead, and only *some* were still alive and waiting the coming of the kingdom of God. Although Mark, like Paul, gave us very little information, what he wrote was consistent with what he would have known had he written in the sixties C.E. when most scholars claim that he composed his gospel. Mark's mention of the *many* for whom Jesus gave his life as a ransom (Mk. 10:45), which is usually taken to be a reference to the Suffering Servant in Isa. 53, may also be an allusion to the auditors of Jesus who died since Jesus was crucified.

The survivors from Jesus' day figured more prominently in the theologies of Paul and Mark than simply as witnesses of the risen Jesus and coming kingdom. If Jesus promised his audience the kingdom, they would not have expected to die before it came. Nor would they have expected to get sick. So Paul was compelled to explain their sickness and death, as a consequence of their partaking of the Lord's Supper unworthily.

> "That is why *many* of you are weak and ill, and *some* have died." (I Cor. 11:30)

Here the proportions are the same as in the above passage (I Cor. 15:6): *many*, though weak and ill, were still alive, and *some* were dead. Apparently, the Lord's Supper was supposed to keep the "Christian" alive and well until the Lord returned. In another letter Paul dealt at length with the problem posed by the premature death of "Christians" (I Thes. 4:13-18). There he claimed that the ones who had died in Christ would rise to join the ones who survived until Christ came.

> "And the dead in Christ will rise first; then *we* who are alive, who are left, shall be caught up together with them in the clouds to meet the Lord in the air; and so we shall always be with the Lord."

By saying ". . . *we* who are alive, who are left . . ." Paul shows that he expected to live until Christ returned.

The death of Jesus' auditors was an issue Paul and Mark had in common: some in the case of Paul and many in the case of Mark. For Paul it was still possible to consider such deaths exceptional and attribute them to a special cause such as the unworthy partaking of the Lord's Supper. However, when Mark wrote his gospel, the problem, which for Paul was peripheral, had become central. Mark had to deal with the unexpected death of most of Jesus' auditors. Apparently, Paul considered baptism and the Lord's Supper as substitutes for death and resurrection. As "Christians" began to die in large numbers, their deaths came to be understood as spirit baptisms. Mark called the prospective deaths of James and John baptisms (Mk 10: 38-40; See also Mk. 1:8).

What was behind this preoccupation with the death of Jesus' auditors? If their deaths came as a surprise that required a special explanation, the unworthy partaking of the Lord's Supper (Paul), then the belief presupposed was that given a worthy participation in the Lord's Supper, they would not have gotten sick and died before the End came. Paul used the example of the wilderness generation in the scriptures to warn the "Christians."

> "For they drank from the spiritual rock that followed them, and the rock was Christ. Nevertheless, God was not pleased with *most* of them, and they were struck down in the wilderness." (I Cor. 10:4-5).

Paul did not expect *most* of Jesus' auditors to die, but they did and Mark used the image of the wilderness generation to make sense of their passing. The exodus generation ate manna (Paul's "supernatural food") in the wilderness and then most of them died. Only a few entered the promised land. Likewise Jesus fed the multitudes in the wilderness and most of them died. Only some would not taste of death until they see the kingdom come in power (Mk. 9:1).

The original form of the belief, which was a function of the belief in the nearness of the end, was that all of Jesus' auditors would live until the kingdom came. Because they interpreted the belief spiritually the gospels of John and Thomas could preserve a more "original" broad form of this belief. John also developed this belief in connection with the example of the wilderness generation.

> "Very truly, I tell you, whoever believes has eternal life. I am the bread of life. Your ancestors ate the manna in the wilderness, and they died. This is the bread that comes down from heaven, so that one may eat of it and not die." (Jn. 6:47-50).

According to John, " . . . whoever believes has eternal life; According to the Gospel of Thomas, "Whoever finds the interpretation of these words shall not taste of death." (Thomas 1:1).

After Jesus and Paul promised their audiences the kingdom of God, the death of their auditors came to be attributed to their lack of holiness (Paul), absence of faith (John), and deficiency of knowledge (gnosis / Thomas). As most of Jesus' generation died, the focus changed from when the kingdom would come to who would live to see it. Just before the Transfiguration mark had Jesus promise the multitude,

> "Truly I tell you, there are some standing here who will not taste of death until they see that the kingdom of God has come with power." (Mk. 9: 1).

Mark may have known of some survivors from Jesus' day, who, he believed, would live to see the kingdom come and then live forever.

By the time Matthew wrote probably all of Jesus' auditors were dead, so he could not simply accept Mark's statement at face value. Matthew retained Mark's saying, revised it, and reversed its meaning. First, he changed Jesus' audience from the multitude to the twelve disciples (Mk. 8: 34 and Matt. 16: 24), which caused the "some standing here" to refer to the three disciples, Peter, James and John, who in the next scene accompanied Jesus up the Mount of Transfiguration, which forged a connection between the two scenes that was not present in Mark. Second, he changed the saying from a promise of seeing the kingdom to one of seeing the "Son of Man" in his kingdom (Mk. 9:1 and Matt. 16:28). This strengthened the link with the Transfiguration scene by focusing attention on seeing Jesus, again creating a common element between the two scenes that did not exist before. Third, to complete the fusion of the two scenes Matthew set about to make changes in the Transfiguration story itself. Mark had only Jesus' garments glow and represented the scene as an objective event; Matthew had Jesus' face shine to connect with the reference to the Son of Man that he had added to the preceding saying and represented the scene as a vision (Mk. 9 and Matt. 17:9). By the time Matthew wrote, all of Jesus' auditors had died and the kingdom had not come in power, so Matthew converted the prophecy that some would live until they saw the kingdom come in power and live forever to a promise that three of Jesus' disciples would see a vision of the Son of Man before they died and they saw him on the mountain.

A second time Jesus said that some of his auditors would live until he returned. When he described the terrible events surrounding the war in Judea, he made clear that he considered them signs of the approaching end.

> "So also, when you see these things taking place, you know that he is near, at the very gate. Truly, I say to you, this generation will not pass away before all things take place." (Mk. 13:29-30).

Among the events Jesus said "this generation" would live to see was " . . . the Son of Man coming in clouds with power and glory." (Mk. 13:26).

Many of Jesus' beliefs, especially the belief in the resurrection, brought him into direct confrontation with the Sadducean priesthood. As if that were not enough, at the Passover season Jesus "cleansed" the Temple and cursed the fig tree, which was a parable hinting at its destruction (Mk. 11: 15-19, and 11: 20-21). When he entered the Temple he invaded the territory of the elite ruling class, " . . . the chief priests and the scribes and the elders . . ." (Mk. 11: 27), who would eventually bring about his death. A series of deadly clashes occurred in rapid succession between Jesus and the ruling elite: They questioned his authority to teach in the Temple; in the Parable of the Vineyard he branded them as murderers; they tried to trick him with the issue of paying taxes to the Romans; the Sadducees, who did not believe in the resurrection, attempted to undermine Jesus' predictions of his resurrection; a scribe posed the popular test question about which was the first commandment; Jesus called into question the Davidic descent of the Messiah; and, finally, defended a poor widow who " . . . out of her poverty has put in everything she had . . ." against the rich people, who " . . . contributed out of their abundance . . ." (Mk. 11: 27-12: 44).

The issue that reveals the most about the interaction of the various factions in Jerusalem at the time is the one about the resurrection. Unlike the Pharisees, the Sadducees had not accepted the newfangled belief in the resurrection, which they claimed was not found in the scriptures. They even argued that a certain provision of the Mosaic law made the notion of resurrection absurd. It had to do with the legal obligation of a man to marry the wife of his deceased brother (Deut. 25: 5). But what if seven brothers died in succession and the woman was wife to all seven. The Sadducee asked, "In the resurrection whose wife will she be?"

In his reply Jesus argued from the scriptures on which the Sadducees had based their argument. He told them they were wrong because they knew " . . . neither the scriptures not the power of God." Jesus prefaced his answer with a reference to angels, another belief which the Sadducees rejected, but Jesus and the Pharisees accepted. Then he presented his argument in the form of an enthymeme or rhetorical syllogism, which has to be reconstructed to see its full form:[55]

> Major premise: God is not the God of the dead but of the living.
> Minor premise: God is the God of Abraham, Isaac, and Jacob.
> Conclusion: Abraham, Isaac, and Jacob must be living.

Mark says a scribe overheard Jesus' debate with the Sadducees. He must have been a scribe of the Pharisees because he approved of Jesus' answer. He also approved of Jesus' answer to his question as to which is the first commandment. Jesus had said to the Sadducees " . . . *you are wrong* . . . ". In deliberate contrast to this, when the scribe heard Jesus' answer, he said,

> "*You are right,* Teacher; you have truly said that he (God) is one, and there is no other but he; and to love him with all the heart, and with all the understanding, and with all the strength, and to love one's neighbor as oneself, is much more than all whole burnt offerings and sacrifices." (Mk. 12: 28-34).

Not only did the scribe summarize a part of the law, a practice frowned upon by the Sadducees, who tended to be "strict constructionists," but also placed love of God and one's neighbor above "burnt offerings and sacrifices," which was the principal occupation of the Sadducean priesthood. Jesus told the scribe that he answered wisely and that he was not far from the kingdom of God. This shows that Jesus—and Mark—rejected the interpretation of scriptures held by the Sadducees, who, Jesus said, knew neither the scriptures not the power of God. We now turn to Jesus' and Mark's interpretation of scriptures, which was closer to that of the scribes of the Pharisees.

"Jesus said to them, 'Is not this the reason you are wrong that you know neither the scriptures nor the power of God?"

(Mk. 12:24).

CHAPTER III

THE SCRIPTURES AND THE POWER OF GOD:
The Scriptural Prophecies of the Passion And Resurrection in Mark

Before the invention of writing, men, like the Sellenites in H.G. Wells" *First Men in the Moon,* had to memorize their entire intellectual tradition. Both Homer's Iliad and much of the Bible were committed to memory and presented orally long before they were written down. Even after the invention of writing, the oral tradition continued to develop alongside the written one. Once a law, poem, or story was reduced to writing, it became inflexible and was sometimes literally etched in stone. The oral tradition revised and updated the written one and kept it relevant and meaningful for the new experiences and circumstances confronted by the heirs of the tradition. When we reach the New Testament era and the Gospel of Mark, the interaction between the oral and written traditions is no longer simple and predictable. Emphasis on the oral tradition in Mark must be qualified by the enormous respect accorded by its author to the written scriptures.

To determine what the oral and written traditions meant for Mark, one must study his vocabulary relative to writing, reading, speaking, and hearing. A casual glance at Mark's use of these terms reveals a remarkable consistency. When he mentioned sources that were written or read, he was almost always referring to the Hebrew scriptures. The sole exception, "Let the reader understand" (Mk. 13:14), may refer to the gospel of Mark itself. Conversely, when Mark pointed to the message that was spoken or heard, he was usually referring to the contemporary message of the gospel. It was only natural for Mark to refer to the scriptures as written or read, but it is noteworthy that he never referred to the individual contemporary stories in his gospel in this manner.

Mark, himself, commented on his dual interest in the past written scriptures and the contemporary oral message. In his answer to the Sadducees Mark's Jesus says "You are ignorant both of the scriptures and the power of God." (Mk. 12:24). In the gospel there is a development from the written scriptures to the oral message to the experienced event. The good news was prophesied in the scriptures, which were written and read, proclaimed in the gospel, which was spoken and heard, and was soon to be demonstrated in power which will be seen and experienced. Some have suggested that the gospel of Mark was written to be read aloud before an audience.[56]

An inspection of the terms Mark used for sources that were written or read reveals a variety that is concealed by our habit of anachronistically attributing all of these references to the Old Testament. In Mark's day there was no Old Testament, just various writings or scriptures. Jack Miles pointed out that the scriptural scrolls were stored in many separate jars that were physically moveable which meant that they were also mentally moveable, preventing them from taking the fixed order they late assumed in the canon.[57] When Mark quoted the scriptures, he did not refer to a single collection of writings, but to several distinct works. His written sources included Isaiah the prophet (Mk. 1:2), Isaiah (Mk. 7:6), scripture (Mk. 12:10), Moses (Mk. 12:19), the scriptures (Mk. 12:24), and scriptures (Mk. 14:49). Three times Mark's Jesus asked his questioners whether they had read: What David did (Mk. 2:25), the scripture (Mk.

12:10), and the book of Moses (Mk. 12:26). Sometimes Mark did not identify his source (Mk. 9:12, 13; 11:17; and 14:21). However, there are only three instances in which he referred to sources as written, but with no quotation following (Mk. 9:12, 13; and 14:21). These last three references merit special attention, which they will receive in this chapter.

If the scriptures were written and read, the gospel (the word) was spoken and heard. In the parables the aural emphasis is unmistakable. The Parable of the Sower, which Jesus delivered orally, was about the word (λόγος), which was heard (Mk. 4:3, 9, 12, 15, 16, 18, 20, 23, 24, and 33). Jesus also called attention to the necessity to hear the word with his repeated warning, "Let anyone with ears to hear listen!" (Mk. 4:9 and 23).

In contrast to the scriptures, which were read, and the gospel, which was heard, the kingdom was to come in power and be seen.

> "Truly, I tell you, there are some standing here who will not taste death until they *see* that the Kingdom of God has come with power." (Mk. 9:1; See also Mk. 14:62).

This visual emphasis is also very prominent in Jesus' farewell discourse on the future (Mk. 13). Concerning Mark 13 Morna Hooker wrote, "The opening warning, Be on guard (βλέπετε), is characteristic of the discourse (cf. v.v. 9, 23, 33). These constant warnings balance the injunctions to hear (ἀκούετε) which punctuate the parables chapter (4: 3, 9, 23, 24, 33; cf. also v. 12)."[58]

Many attempts have been made to determine what Mark's sources were and how he edited them. We can be certain that Mark used one group of written sources, to which we have independent access—the scriptures. We can determine with a great deal of accuracy what these sources were and how Mark edited them. Editorial or redaction principles based on sources that first have to be reconstructed hypothetically are on much shakier grounds. Therefore, we will begin with a consideration of the scriptural "prophecies," of Jesus' death and resurrection in Mark.

Over two hundred years ago Anthony Collins, the English Deist, argued that the Old Testament prophecies cited in the New Testament, if taken literally, were not fulfilled. He maintained that there was a lack of correspondence between the prophecies in the Old Testament and the supposed fulfilling events in the New Testament. In order to effect an agreement between the two, Collins said that the New Testament writers interpreted the Old Testament prophecies in a secondary typical, mystical, allegorical or enigmatical sense.[59] The very first prophecy quoted by Mark presents us with a problem of correspondence that is not unlike that noticed by Collins. The gospel of Mark begins with the passage from Isaiah about the messenger who cried, "Prepare the way of the Lord!" (Mk. 1:2-3). Nowhere did Mark have John the Baptist say precisely these words. Nor did the prophecy make explicit reference to the death of John the Baptist or Jesus.

This apparent lack of correspondence between the messenger prophecy and the gospel story led scholars to prefer instead the passage about the Suffering Servant in Isaiah 53, which contained the required imagery of suffering. To use Isaiah 53 to illustrate Jesus' sufferings scholars had to overcome the objection that Mark not only did not introduce his gospel with that passage, but also failed to quote it anywhere else in his gospel. Although Isaiah 53 could have portrayed the motif of Jesus' suffering in Mark, it could not have illustrated the equally important theme of his resurrection in that gospel.

Since historians were more interested in the historical Jesus, than in the gospel story, Mark's failure to mention Isaiah 53 was not a fatal blow to their enterprise. They considered Jesus' death the most certain fact of his life, and regarded Mark's emphasis on Jesus' suffering and death a more or less accurate reflection of the actual events. In their view it was Jesus—not Mark—who was influenced by Isaiah 53. The historical study of Mark produced a fairly broad consensus that Jesus understood his impending death in accordance with the notion of the Suffering Servant in Isaiah 53. In his thorough study of the subject C. R. North wrote,

> "It is almost universally admitted that Jesus saw his way by the light that Isa. liii shed upon His predestined path."[60]

Historians regarded Isaiah 53, which explained how Jesus came to embrace his mission of suffering and death, from a psychological and historical rather than a theological or literary viewpoint. They could argue that Jesus referred to Isaiah 53, or even quoted the passage, only to have his auditors fail to report it. After all, it was precisely the suffering and death of Jesus that occasioned so much misunderstanding among his followers.

However, Mark's failure to quote Isaiah 53 cannot be accounted for in this way. If the Suffering Servant passage had been uppermost in Mark's mind, it should have been foremost in his gospel, a place conspicuously occupied by an entirely different passage about the messenger who cried in the desert (Mk. 1:2-3). A procedure that may have been justified in a historical study of Jesus should not have been transferred to a literary study of Mark without considerable qualification. Frequently, literary critics simply took over the observations made by historians and turned them into literary observations. In my opinion a thorough-going literary criticism will affect not only the form of the story but also its content.

When attention shifted from the Jesus of history to the Jesus of the gospel story, Isaiah 53 was already available to account for Mark's portrayal of the suffering Son of Man.

Two examples will show how literary critics took over this application of Isaiah 53 to the historical Jesus and applied it to the story of Jesus' sufferings in Mark. In a literary study of Mark, in which he compared the gospel to Greek tragedy, Curtis Beach wrote,

> "Both the Passion story and this 'suffering service' sequence show the influence of the 'suffering servant' poem in Isaiah 53. Mark has Jesus move toward his death 'like a lamb that is led to the slaughter' (Isa. 53:7)."[61]

In a more recent literary and theological study of Mark, James G. Williams wrote,

> "The suffering servant of the Lord is the most important of these scriptural types, and it in turn is married to the apocalyptic Son of Man, who gives the Servant a more potent and inclusive future dimension."[62]

Given these claims for the unique importance of Isaiah 53 for Mark, one could reasonably expect to find the Suffering Servant passage quoted at the beginning of the gospel.

The literary approach to the gospel requires that one consider the scriptural prophecies that Mark quoted and applied to Jesus' death and resurrection before one searches the scriptures for other passion and resurrection prophecies. There are at least three such prophecies in Mark: the messenger prophecy (Mk. 1:2-3); the cornerstone prophecy (Mk. 12:10-11); and the smitten shepherd prophecy (Mk. 14:27-28). Since the messenger prophecy is the least obvious passion and resurrection prophecy, it will require an extended explanation, which is also justified by its emphatic position at the beginning of Mark, and its apparent programmatic character.

As it is Written: The Messenger Prophecy as the Primary Passion and Resurrection Prophecy in Mark (Mk. 1:2-3)

That the messenger prophecy referred to the Lord, whose way was prepared by John the Baptist, suggests that the prophecy was also related to the story of Jesus and not just to the story of John. That being the case, one could reasonably expect to find references to the prophecy distributed throughout the gospel where I will contend they are found at the beginning (Mk. 1:2-3), middle (Mk. 9:11-13), and end of Mark (Mk. 14:21).

Mark quoted the messenger prophecy at the beginning of the gospel.

> "The beginning of the good news of Jesus Christ, the Son of God. As it is written in the prophet Isaiah,
> See I am sending my messenger ahead of you,
> who will prepare your way;
> the voice of one crying out in the wilderness:
> 'Prepare the way of the Lord,
> make his paths straight,'" (Mk. 1:1-3)

When Mark first explicitly identified John and Jesus as Elijah and the Son of Man, he had Jesus allude to the Messenger Prophecy with a quotation formula but without quoting the passage again.

> "As they were coming down the mountain, he ordered them to tell no one about what they had seen, until after the Son of Man had risen from the dead. So they kept the matter to themselves, questioning what this rising from the dead could mean. Then they asked him, 'Why do the scribes say that Elijah must come first?' He said to them, 'Elijah is indeed coming first to restore all things. How then

is it written about the Son of Man, that he is to go through many sufferings and be treated with contempt? But I tell you that Elijah has come, and they did to him whatever they pleased, as it is written about him.'" (Mk. 9:9-13).

Finally, in the passion story Mark had Jesus refer to the same prophecy again. Once more Jesus used only the quotation formula without quoting the scripture that he had in mind.

> "For the Son of Man goes *as it is written of him*, but woe to that one by whom the Son of Man is betrayed." (Mk. 14:21)"

In order to establish this rather bold assertion I will begin with a discussion of the prophecy, itself, and the usual approach to it.

The Messenger Prophecy at the beginning of Mark: (Mk. 1:2-3)

It is customary to interpret the Messenger Prophecy analytically calling attention to its composite character, Old Testament origin, and application to John the Baptist. Typical of this approach is Howard Clark Kee's claim,

> " . . . that through Jesus' baptism at the hand of John were fulfilled both the promises of an eschatological messenger (Mal. 3:1) and the announcement of the one who would prepare for the Lord's coming (Isa. 40:3)."[63]

While the prophecy referred to John the Baptist, it was not his way but the Lord's that John prepared. So, presumably, the theme of the way would become central in the story only after the Lord arrived on the scene.

The analytical approach was in evidence in the frequent observation that the entire prophecy was erroneously attributed to Isaiah by Mark, a mistake because part of the prophecy came from Malachi (Mal. 3:1), and Exodus (Exo. 23:20). Anyone who is tempted to use this example to illustrate our modern critical view of the gospels might be surprised to discover that Jerome in the fourth century had already observed that the words,

> "'Behold I send before you my angel (messenger) who will prepare the way for you' are found at the end of Malachi and not in Isaiah." Jerome drew the logical conclusion, "O Apostle Peter, your son Mark, son in the Spirit not in the flesh, expert in spiritual matters, has made a mistake here."[64]

The text on which the King James Version was based got rid of the difficulty by simply correcting the introductory verse to read "in the prophets" instead of "in the prophet Isaiah." Matthew and Luke solved the problem by striking the reference to the messenger in Malachi (Matt. 3:3; Lu. 3:4-6; and Mal. 3:1), and locating it elsewhere (Matt. 11:10; Lk. 7:27).

If we look for the antecedents of even the most highly structured work, we can discover the elements out of which it was composed. These independent parts, which existed prior to the form given to them by the artist, should not control our interpretation of the completed work unless they also guided its composition. Whether he found the composite prophecy in his sources or combined the passages himself and mistakenly attributed them to Isaiah, as Jerome thought, Mark evidently considered these scriptures particularly appropriate to the message that he wished to convey.

If one views the prophecy not in terms of its antecedents, but in terms of its consequences in the overall structure of Mark, one must begin with the form that the prophecy assumed in the gospel of Mark. Without denying its composite character, one needs to ask how the Markan form of the prophecy is related to the gospel story. By concentrating on the elements out of which the prophecy was composed, interpreters have ignored the shape that it took in Mark, which placed the proclaimer in the desert where Jesus subsequently taught and fed the multitudes. The passage in Isaiah had said that the way should be prepared in the desert not that the message would be proclaimed there.

> "A voice cries out: 'In the wilderness prepare the way of the Lord make straight in the desert a highway for our God.'" (Isa. 40:3)

The passage is in the form of a synonymous parallelism, in which the second verset repeated the thought of the first verset. The "wilderness" corresponded to the "desert," "prepare" to "make straight," and "the Lord" to "our God." Robert Alter pointed out that such parallelisms were not exactly synonymous.[65] While the first verset called for a general preparation of the way, the second verset specified that this preparation involved making straight a highway.

According to Mark not only was the way prepared in the desert, but the message was proclaimed there as well. In order to place the messenger in the desert, the proclaimer had to appear in both versets, so Mark, or the tradition he used, created a new parallelism with precisely that result.

> "See, I am sending my *messenger* ahead of you, who will prepare your way; t*he voice* of one crying out in the wilderness: Prepare the way of the Lord, Make his paths straight . . ." (Mk. 1:2-3).

The "messenger: of the first verset corresponded to the "the voice" of the second verset, which clearly placed the proclaimer of the message in the desert. There are also other important differences between Mark's version of the prophecy and Isaiah's. In Isaiah "the voice" spoke the prophecy; in Mark God, the "I" of the first verse, uttered it. When "the voice" spoke the prophecy, the way was prepared for the Lord God (Isaiah); when God uttered the prophecy, the way was prepared for the Lord Jesus (Mark).

The Messenger Prophecy in the Middle and End of Mark (Mk. 9:11-13 and 14:21)

Joel Marcus claimed that when Mark used a quotation formula, but did not quote a specific scripture, he was expressing "an exegetical conclusion, and "did not have a particular Old Testament text in mind."[66] In contrast I will maintain that each time Mark used the quotation formula by itself, he had in mind a specific scriptural passage, which he had previously cited. In the first half of the gospel, Mark introduced John the Baptist and Jesus with the messenger prophecy, which began with the quotation formula, "As it is written in Isaiah the prophet;" (Mk. 1:2). In the second half of the gospel, Mark introduced Elijah and the Son of Man with the quotation formula alone, "how then is it written," and "as it is written about him" (Mk. 9:12-13).

In my opinion Mark did not quote the scripture again because he thought that it would be obvious to his hearers / readers what passage he had in mind. There were at least two possibilities: Mark thought that the prophecy intended would easily come to the hearers'/readers' mind either because the imagery employed in it corresponded to the fulfilling event, or because he had already quoted the prophecy in connection with John and Jesus in the preceding narrative. Scholars have usually opted for the first alternative. It was just such a correspondence in imagery between the Suffering Servant in Isaiah and suffering Son of Man in Mark that led so many scholars to choose Isaiah 53 as the primary passion prophecy in Mark.

However, since Isaiah 53 did not mention the suffering of John the Baptist, scholars were forced to look for a second prophecy. The expectation of a correspondence between the prophecy and fulfilling event governed Vincent Taylor's search for such a prophecy. Taylor suggested that Mark was referring to the threats that Jezebel made against the historical Elijah (1 Ki. 19:2, 10).[67] The same presupposition led D. E. Nineham to state emphatically, "The Old Testament contains no suggestion that Elijah when he returned would be rejected."[68] Similarly, Howard Clark Kee asserted emphatically, " . . . no known Jewish writing contains such a prophecy."[69] of the suffering Son of Man. He assumed that the scriptures would have to have contained such a prophecy for the early Christians to have found it there, a dubious assumption.

A few pages earlier Kee gave the correct rationale for searching for the scripture that Mark had in mind, " . . . the New Testament writers exercised an embarrassing degree of freedom in applying an Old Testament text to their situation."[70] Then he referred to the discomfiture of the modern interpreter when confronted with what the New Testament claimed " . . . to have happened 'according to the scriptures.' "[71] Here no correspondence in imagery was required. On the contrary, it was precisely the lack of such correspondence that so confounded our historically trained and literal minded interpreter.

By prefacing the story of John the Baptist and Jesus with the messenger prophecy, Mark retrospectively defined "the way in the desert" as the way of suffering. Just as the messenger prophecy introduced the activities of John and Jesus (Mk. 1:2-3), the unspecified scripture (Mk. 9:11-13) announced the sufferings of Elijah and the Son of Man. Mark did not feel the need to inform the reader explicitly that the unspecified scripture was the messenger prophecy, because it was the only scriptural passage in Mark that referred to both John the Baptist and Jesus. If Mark had meant to refer to two different passages, it would have been necessary for him to have indicated which scripture was intended for John and which for Jesus.

In order to demonstrate which passage Mark had in mind we must first understand how he quoted scripture. We are so used to citing scripture by chapter and verse that we overlook certain specific features of the ancient method. For example, when Jesus answered the Sadducees, he said, "As for the dead being raised, have you not read in the book of Moses, in the story about the bush, . . ." (Mk. 12:26). According to Morna Hooker, "This method of referring to a particular passage by a key phrase (here lit. 'at the bush') was the normal one at the time, since chapter and verse divisions were unknown."[72] Just such a key phrase was used in the passage we have been discussing. While no quotation followed the introductory formula, "As it is written about him," a key phrase reference preceded it, namely, "to restore all things," a reference to Malachi 4:5 and 6, and Mark 1:2 and 3. In my opinion the introductory formula refers to the same passages.

Analysis of the passage in question (Mk. 9:9-13) leads to the same conclusion. Two observations have derailed attempts to interpret this scene correctly: scholars' overriding interest in the suffering theme and Wrede's theory which focused on the mention of the resurrection. There may be some truth to Wrede's theory and certainly Mark was interested in the suffering theme, but neither was the main subject of this passage. The reference to the resurrection merely served to provoke the discussion and the mention of suffering was a subordinate element, which was designed to identify John and Jesus with Elijah and the Son of Man.

The entire discussion that followed revolved around the question as to whether it were necessary for Elijah to come first. The disciples asked Jesus why the scribes say Elijah must come first. In his reply Jesus answered the disciples by twice referring to the coming of Elijah: "Elijah is indeed coming first" and "Elijah has come." These two references to the coming first of Elijah form a parallelism that frames a reference to the suffering of the Son of Man. The parallelism may be exhibited as follows:

> "Elijah is indeed coming first to restore all things."
> "Elijah has come and they did to him whatever they pleased, as it is written about him." (Mk. 9:12 and 13).

Since the two statements about Elijah are parallel, the reference to scripture, "as it is written about him," refers to both statements. Mark could have written, "Elijah is indeed coming first to restore all things as it is written about him." If he had done so, the scriptural reference would have been transparent. It is also clear that the phrase, "as it is written about him," referred to Elijah's coming first as well as his suffering because the two elements are joined by the coordinating conjunction, "and" (kai): "Elijah has come, *and* kai) they did to him whatever they pleased." The passages in the Old Testament that referred to the coming of Elijah are the ones that Mark quoted at the beginning of the gospel (Mk. 1:2, 3).

Not only does the internal analysis of the above passage suggest that it refers to the Messenger Prophecy, but also the relationship between the messenger prophecy and the rest of the gospel leads to the same conclusion. The messenger prophecy is connected with the entire gospel story and not just the career of John the Baptist. If John prepared the way and Jesus did not travel on it, it was a road leading nowhere. Recent studies of Mark have shown that a number of elements of the prophecy appeared throughout the gospel, which strengthens the case for finding references to the prophecy later in Mark. At least two themes linked the messenger prophecy with the rest of the gospel: the desert and the way.

The Desert as a Symbol of Death and Resurrection

According to Willi Marxsen, the reference to the desert in the story of John the Baptist (Mk. 1:4) was derived from the messenger prophecy (Mk. 1:3); it was a theological concept rather than a geographical fact.[73] Ulrich Mauser went one step further and linked up the references to the "desert place" elsewhere in Mark with its mention in the prophecy (Mk. 1:3, 4, 12, 13, 35, 45; 6:31, 32, 35; and 8:4).[74] The same Greek work (ερήμος) was used in all of these instances. Not only was John the Baptist in the desert, but also Jesus, and not just when John baptized him, but also when he fed the multitude. However, Mauser's attempt to extend the desert motif to the second half of Mark merely highlighted the fact that it appeared only in the first half of the gospel. The continuation of the desert theme in the first half of Mark demonstrated that there is a connection between the prophecy and that part of the gospel.

The location of the desert in Galilee is difficult to square with geographical facts. Josephus, the Jewish historian, who was the governor of Galilee and very well acquainted with the region, described its fertility in glowing terms.

> "The whole area is excellent for crops or cattle and rich in forests of every kind, so that by its adaptability it invites even those least inclined to work on the land. Consequently every inch has been cultivated by the inhabitants and not a corner goes to waste."[75]

The translators of the Revised Standard Version recognized

the problem and rendered the Greek word for desert (ερημος) variously as "wilderness" (Mk. 1:3, 4, 12, 13), "a lonely place" (Mk. 1:35; 6:31, 32, 35), "the country" (Mk. 1:45), and "desert" (Mk. 8:4).

To understand how Mark could refer to Galilee as a desert one must take into account the difference between the ancient and modern conceptions of a desert. Whereas we distinguish fertile regions from desert areas, the ancients contrasted the condition of even fertile areas during the different seasons. In other words they considered even fertile land in winter a virtual desert. The alternation of seasons with the waning and waxing of vegetation they believed to result from the death and resurrection of the God. The rejuvenated desert in Isaiah (Isa. 43:19-20) and the desert in Mark in which there is green grass (Mk. 6:39) can easily represent resurrection.

In addition to the primitive notion of the desert, which made it such an appropriate symbol of death and resurrection, Mark may also have had in mind a historical example. Jesus' feeding of the multitudes in the desert has reminded many commentators of God's feeding Israel in the wilderness in the Old Testament.[76] The feeding of Israel in the desert was celebrated in poetry as an example of God's mercy, and as an example of what happens to people who rebel against God. Concerning the wilderness generation the psalmist wrote,

> "Mortals ate of the bread of angels;
> he sent them food in abundance." (Psa. 78:25)

> "In spite of all this they still sinned; they did not
> believe in his wonders.
> So he made their days vanish like a breath,
> And their years in terror." (Psa. 78: 32-33)

Paul, a contemporary of Mark, also wrote about the wilderness generation.

> "Nevertheless, God was not pleased with most of them, and they were struck down in the wilderness. Now these things occurred as example for us, so that we might not desire evil as they did." (1 Cor. 10:5-6).

The author of Hebrews also made use of the wilderness generation as a warning and example.

> "Now who were they who heard and yet were rebellious? Was it not all those who left Egypt under the leadership of Moses? But with whom was he angry forty years? Was it not those who sinned, whose bodies fell in the wilderness? And to whom did he swear that they would not enter his rest, if not to those who were disobedient? So we see that they were unable to enter because of unbelief. Therefore, while the promise of entering his rest is still open, let us take care that none of you should seem to have failed to reach it." (Heb. 3: 16-4: 1; compare Psa. 95: 8-11).

After the Israelites left Egypt, they wandered in the desert for forty years. Most of them died in the desert leaving only a few to enter the promised land with the new generation. Mark placed the generation that heard Jesus speak in the desert, because, like the Exodus generation, only some of them did not taste of death before they realized the promised salvation (Mk. 9:1). Also, like the Exodus generation, the multitudes in Mark were fed in the desert before they died. As the death of Moses was connected with the death of the Exodus generation, the death of Jesus was associated with the demise of the new Exodus generation of the End time. It will soon become evident how pervasive the theme of Jesus's death is in the feeding stories. It is the desert theme that leads up to the first allusion to the messenger prophecy (Mk. 9:11-13).

The Way as a Symbol of Death and Resurrection

A theme that connected the messenger prophecy with the story of Jesus' death was that of "the way." Ambrozic expressed the matter cautiously,

> "... yet it may not be entirely false to see in the 'way' of 1:2 an anticipation of the typically Marcan En Te Hodos (in the way) which occurs later in the Gospel mostly in redactionally formed verses."[77]

The same author went on to show that John's preparation of the way consisted in more than preaching; it also included his dying.

Mark defined "the way" as the way of suffering not only by using the expression to introduce the passions of John and Jesus, but also by distributing the term throughout the story of Jesus' death. The phrase "the way" was clearly a passion symbol because it was more prominent in the second half of the gospel, which dealt with Jesus' death (Mk. 1:2, 3; 2:33; 4:4, 15; 6:8; 8:3, 27; 9:33, 34; 10:17, 32, 46, 52; 11:8 and 12:14). Therefore, Kelber was not justified when he made "the way" refer also to Jesus' Galilean ministry.[78] At least he ought to have recognized and explained the relative scarcity of the term in the first half of Mark.

Once again, a theme, which began in the programmatic prophecy at the beginning of Mark is continued in the second half of the gospel. Just as the "desert" motif led up to the first allusion to the messenger prophecy, the "way" theme ends in still another reference to the same prophecy (Mk. 14:21). It has not gone unnoticed that the reference to the passion of the Son of Man, "As it is written about him ..." (Mk. 14:21) assumes precisely the same form as the reference to the passion of Elijah (Mk. 9:13).[79] The phrase "as it is written," with no quotation following, functions as a counterpart to the modern author's *Ibid*, or *op cit*. So there are references to the messenger prophecy at the beginning (Mk. 1: 2-3), middle (Mk. 9: 11-13), and end of Mark (Mk. 14:21).

In the light of the above observations it is incumbent upon us to ask whether other elements of the messenger prophecy are continued in the rest of the gospel. Of course, the messenger / voice is to be understood as John / Elijah, and the Lord as Jesus / Son of Man. There may even be a terminological continuation of the Greek word ευθείας, straight, in the frequently used Markan expression, ευθύς, straightway. In Greek these two words (ευθείας and ευθύς) were related much like their English counterparts (straight and straightway). This parallelism of terms is obscured by the current translation of ευθύς by immediately, since translation of the associated Greek term, ευθείας, by immediate, instead of straight, though possible would be awkward. On a way that has been made straight, one can accomplish things straightway.

Mark's use of the term ευθύς, immediately, some 40 times, which suggests the forward rush of events, is balanced by his use of the word πάλιν, again, which directs the attention to preceding events. It was once thought that the term was used arbitrarily like some nervous habit of oral speech such as "you know." It is now known that Mark used the term quite deliberately with specific antecedents in mind. In the third prediction of Jesus' death Mark says "And he took *again* (πάλιν), the twelve . . .," and predicted the death of the Son of Man, which raises the question, when did he predict his death before? Of course, we know that he predicted his death on two previous occasions (Mk. 8:31 and 9:31).[80]

The Messenger Prophecy and the Twofold Structure of Mark

Not only did the repetition of terms from the messenger prophecy in the rest of the gospel support the theory about allusions to it later in Mark, but also the twofold structure of the gospel provided the framework for the allusions to the prophecy. The detailed argument for the two-part structure of Mark will be presented in chapter four; here it will be dealt with only briefly in relation to the allusions to the messenger prophecy.

Mark told the gospel story twice: first using the names John and Jesus and then using the names Elijah and the Son of Man. In other words John the Baptist was the forerunner of Jesus in the first half of Mark (Mk. 1:1-4), and Elijah was the precursor of the Son of Man in the second half of the gospel (Mk. 9: 11-13). The implication is obvious: If the messenger prophecy belonged with the story of John the Baptist and Jesus, it also belonged with the story of Elijah and the Son of Man. Mark told the story of John and Jesus just after he quoted the messenger prophecy; he began to tell the story of Elijah and the Son of Man in a dialogue between Jesus and three of his disciples. This second telling of the story took the form of a backward glance at the activity of John the Baptist (Mk. 9: 11-13). Since Jesus' reflection on the career of John recapitulated his mission of restoring all things, it is reasonable to assume that the allusion to the prophecy (Mk. 9: 11-13) also referred to something in the preceding narrative, namely, the messenger prophecy at the beginning of Mark (Mk. 1: 2-3).

Now it is clear why Mark did not think that it was necessary to quote the messenger prophecy each time that he referred to it: he expected the redundant structure of the story to suggest to the reader what scripture he had in mind. Elements missing in the second telling of the story could easily be filled in from the first version.

Our discussion of the messenger prophecy has attempted to do justice to its programmatic character, and emphatic location at the beginning of Mark. Mark did not expect the reader or hearer to forget it as he read or heard the rest of the gospel. Like stage scenery in a play, the "way" and the "desert" formed the backdrop against which the rest of the gospel events were to be viewed. That Mark merely alluded to the prophecy in the middle and end of the gospel only showed the extent to which he presupposed the lingering image of the way in the desert in the mind of the reader or listener.[81] In addition to the messenger prophecy Mark quoted at least two other prophecies of the death and resurrection of Jesus: the cornerstone prophecy (Mk. 12:10-11), and the smitten shepherd prophecy (Mk. 14:27-28).

The Cornerstone Prophecy

After relating the Parable of the Vineyard, Jesus said,

> "Have you not read this scripture: 'The very stone which the builders rejected has become the head of the corner; this was the Lord's doing and it is marvelous in our eyes'?" (Mk. 12: 10-11; Psa. 118:22-23).

Mark required a prophecy that not only mentioned death and resurrection, but also contained a communal dimension. There were three passions in Mark: John's, Jesus' and Mark's community. Although the Suffering Servant in Isaiah 53 may originally have been a communal image of suffering, scholars obviously chose it to represent the suffering of an individual, Jesus. In contrast the prophecies that Mark chose included a reference to the community: the rejected stone became the cornerstone of a new temple, which represented the community, and the smitten shepherd, after his resurrection, led his sheep, the community, into Galilee. Likewise, Jesus' own predictions of his death and resurrection (Mk. 8: 31, 9: 31, and 10: 33-34), were immediately followed by teachings about the suffering in store for his disciples and followers (Mk. 8: 34-38; 9: 35-37, and 10: 35-45). Therefore, Jesus' predictions conformed to the pattern set by the Old Testament prophecies that Mark chose to represent the death and resurrection of Jesus. In fact there is a terminological link between the first prediction of the passion and resurrection, in which the Son of Man was "rejected" (ἀποδοκιμασθῆναι), (Mk. 8:31) and the cornerstone prophecy, in which the stone was "rejected" (ἀπεδοκίμασαν) (Mk. 12:10).

The prophecies that Mark selected "predicted," not only Jesus' death, but also his resurrection. If the stone were rejected (Jesus' death), it would later become the cornerstone (Jesus' resurrection). Since the Smitten Shepherd prophecy made no mention of the sheep being gathered together again after being scattered, and contained no reference to Jesus' resurrection, Mark added a prophecy of Jesus to make these points: "But after I am raised up, I will go before you to Galilee." Jesus' passion and resurrection predictions conformed to this same pattern in that they mentioned both his death and resurrection.

If these Old Testament passages functioned as genuine prophecies in Mark, one would expect to find allusions to the prophecies in the fulfilling events. The immediate context of the cornerstone prophecy was the Parable of the Vineyard in which the opponents of Jesus were portrayed as tenants of a vineyard, who killed the owner's son in order to get control of the property. Instead, the owner of the vineyard took the property from them and gave it to others (the gentiles). The accompanying cornerstone prophecy pictured the Jewish leaders as incompetent builders who rejected the stone that became the cornerstone of a new building. If the tenant's killing of the son led to their loss of the vineyard, then the builder's rejection of the unrecognized cornerstone led to the destruction of their building, the Temple!

Mark's explicit anti-Temple polemic began with the stories of Jesus' cursing the fig tree and cleansing the temple (Mk. 11: 12-19). Mark juxtaposed the two stories in such a way as to imply that the cleansed Temple would wither like the cursed fig tree.[82] When Jesus gave the apocalyptic timetable for the rejection of the Jewish leadership, he described the destruction of the Temple, in which not one stone would be left upon another (Mk. 13: 2).

In his account of the Jewish trial of Jesus, Mark returned to the Temple building imagery:

> "And some stood up and bore false witness against him, saying, We heard him say, 'I will destroy this temple that is made with hands, and in three days I will build another, not made with hand.'" (Mk. 14: 57-58).

Again, while Jesus died on the cross,

> "... those who passed by derided him, wagging their heads, and saying, 'aha! You who would destroy the temple and build it in three day ...'" (Mk. 15: 29)

Mark characterized the testimony of the witnesses as "false witness," but it appeared to contain a clear reference to Jesus' death and resurrection. Even the three days were mentioned. So in what sense was their witness false? Of course, it was literally false in the sense that Mark never had Jesus say that he would destroy the Temple; its destruction was caused by the builder's rejection of the corner stone. However, there was another sense in which their witness may be considered as false. If the saying were taken to be a prophecy of Jesus' death and resurrection, the witnesses were wrong to consider it a reference to the destruction of the actual Temple. The gospel of John attributed a similar saying to Jesus and gave it an interpretation very close to the meaning of Mark,

> "Jesus answered them, 'Destroy this temple, and in three days I will raise it up.' The Jews then said, 'It

> has taken forty-six years to build this temple, and will you raise it up in three days?' but he spoke of the temple of his body." (Jn. 2: 19-21).

In my opinion the misunderstanding of Jesus' accusers in Mark was very similar to that of the Jews in John; both interpreted the saying literally instead of symbolically as it was intended.

The curtain fell on Mark's anti-Temple polemic (so to speak) when the curtain of the Temple " . . . was torn in two, from top to bottom." (Mk. 15: 38). The confession of the centurion followed immediately, "Truly this man was the Son of God." (Mk. 15: 39). The gentiles had just inherited the vineyard from the beloved son and heir. The stone that would become the cornerstone of a new Temple had just been rejected. The author of the Deutero-Pauline Ephesians spoke of this new Temple as one,

> " . . . built upon the foundation of the apostles and prophets, Christ Jesus himself being the cornerstone, in whom the whole structure is joined together and grows into a holy temple in the Lord;" (Eph. 2:20-21).

The Smitten Shepherd Prophecy

When mark repeated the story of John the Baptist and Jesus using the names Elijah and the son of Man, he merely alluded to the introductory messenger prophecy with a quotation formula, but with no quotation. He used the same technique when he referred to the smitten shepherd prophecy. According to Mark, Jesus said to his disciples,

> "You will all fall away; for it is written 'I will strike the shepherd, and the sheep will be scattered.' But after

> I am raised up, I will go before you to Galilee." (Mk. 14: 27-28; Zech. 13: 7).

When the first part of this prophecy was fulfilled, it was merely alluded to, and not quoted. When Jesus was arrested, he said,

> "But let the scriptures be fulfilled." Mark added, "And they all forsook him and fled." (Mk. 14: 49-50).

The comment of Mark showed that the reference to scriptures (sic) was an allusion to the one about the shepherd being smitten and the sheep scattered that he had just quoted in the preceding narrative. The prophecy also applied to the next story in Mark about the young man who ran away naked when Jesus was seized (Mk. 14: 51-52). The two stories shared a common Greek Term for fleeing: the disciples fled (εΦυγον), and the young man fled (εΦυγεν). Marvin Meyers noticed the relationship between the fleeing disciples and fleeing young man, but failed to notice the connection with Jeremiah's prophecy.[83] Allusions to the smitten shepherd prophecy continued throughout the story of Jesus' death. In the story of Jesus' trial and crucifixion there were three references to the prophecy: At the Jewish trial the guards and others struck Jesus, Pilate had him scourged, and the soldiers hit him on the head just before they crucified him. (Mk. 14: 65; 15: 15, 19).

By placing Jesus' prediction of Peter's denial after the smitten shepherd prophecy, Mark made Peter a symbol of the scattered sheep. Mark also associated the events fulfilling the two predictions. In a clear allusion to the smitten shepherd prophecy Mark wrote,

> "and some began to spit on him, and to cover his face, and to strike him, saying to him, 'prophesy!' And the guards received him with blows." (Mk. 14: 65).

The very next scene was the story of Peter's denial (Mk. 14: 66-72).

When "some" struck Jesus, they ordered him to prophesy, which was probably intended ironically because their very blows fulfilled Jesus / Zechariah's prophecy about the smitten shepherd. Matthew overlooked Mark's irony, focused too narrowly on the immediate context, became preoccupied with the problem of what Jesus was supposed to prophesy, and took it to be the identity of the one who struck him.

> "Then they spat in his face, and *struck* him; and some *slapped* him, saying, 'Prophesy to us, you Christ! Who is it that *struck* you?'" (Matt. 26: 67-68)

Matthew's preoccupation with the problem of what was to be prophesied was revealed in his threefold reference to "striking," one of which displaced the blindfolding of Jesus which was mentioned by Mark.

Luke accepted Matthew's solution, but may have noticed that the latter's omission of Mark's reference to the blindfolding of Jesus created still another problem: it would not necessarily have taken prophetic gifts for Jesus to have "prophesied" who struck him unless he was blindfolded. Therefore, Luke put the blindfold back on Jesus.

> "Now the men who were holding Jesus mocked him and beat him; they also blindfolded him and asked him 'Prophesy! Who is it that struck you?'" (Lk. 22: 63-64).

William Farmer, who considered Matthew the earliest gospel, also had trouble with the missing blindfold in that gospel. According to Farmer, Matthew " . . . pictured Jesus with other men's spittle running down his face and buffeted by their blows, being so distracted by this abuse he could only with difficulty have identified those who had struck him."[84] It is obvious that Farmer went to great lengths to construct a substitute for the missing blindfold in Matthew.

This leaves one remaining problem: the meaning of the blindfold in Mark. Since Mark did not have Jesus' captors ask him to prophesy who struck him, the blindfolding appears to be without purpose. However, when Mark had Jesus blindfolded, it recalls to mind the symbolical healing of the blind men in that gospel (Mk. 8: 22-26; 10: 46-52). There are also a great deal of sayings in Mark about seeing and not seeing (Mk. 4: 12, 8: 18). Perhaps, Mark meant to imply that Jesus could see more blindfolded than his captors could see with their eyes wide open. At least this interpretation is consistent with the ironic sense of the passage.

The second part of the smitten shepherd prophecy about the sheep (disciples) being gathered together in Galilee was repeated at the end of Mark. The young man at the tomb told the women to

" . . . go, tell his disciples and Peter that he is going before you to Galilee; there you will see him, as he told you." (Mk. 16:7).

Mark singled out Peter not only when the sheep were scattered, but also when they were gathered together again. If Peter never got the message or did not act on his original hearing of the prophecy (a possibility which is not usually considered), then a prophecy of Jesus would have remained unfulfilled, a thing unthinkable for Mark.

Conclusion

We now return to the problem raised by Anthony Collins, namely, that of the lack of correspondence between the scriptural "prophecies" literally understood and the supposed fulfilling event in the New Testament. While it is necessary for us to acknowledge the disjunction between "Old

Testament prophecies" and New Testament events, it is also incumbent upon us to try to understand how Mark and other New Testament writers connected the two. Collins has proven to be a reliable guide in this matter also when he suggested that early Christian methods of interpretation were based on preceding Jewish ones. His observation has been confirmed by the Dead Sea Scrolls. Norman Perrin claimed,

> "... that the New Testament tradition does do exactly what the Qumran pesher tradition does: it understands and interprets events within its own experience and aspects of its own expectation in the light of Old Testament passages, and in so doing it exercises significant freedom with regard to the wording of the Old Testament passage concerned."[85]

To describe the method pursued by the New Testament writers Collins used a number of terms which he treated as synonyms: secondary, typical, mystical, or allegorical, or enigmatical.[86] With its two levels of meaning, literal and spiritual, allegory provided the means of connecting the two testaments. In fact allegory could connect almost anything with anything else: the prophecy with its fulfillment, the parable with its interpretation, and the first half of Mark with the second half of the gospel. Its arbitrary character was overlooked because of the importance of what it accomplished by rescuing a tradition which otherwise at best would have been irrelevant and at worst meaningless. Lacking the concept of historical development, many great thinkers have turned to allegory to make sense of the past: Collins, Bunyan, Augustine, Origen, and Mark. Strauss connected the scriptural prophecies and the fulfilling events by means of the notion of myth, which allowed for the influence of the Old Testament on the New mediated by the early Christian consciousness.

In addition to the individual stories, which have been described as allegories or myths, Mark told an overarching story for which he utilized a medium that is common to reporters of fact and fiction, namely, narrative. The psychologist, Janet, maintained that normal human memory takes the form of a story, which includes beliefs and feelings as well as facts.[87] With the development of the English novel, literary criticism has devised methods for dealing with large scale narratives such as the Gospel of Mark. As we can see, the history of interpretation has left us with a lot of baggage to unpack before we can decide what kind of story Mark told. We will set the stage for presenting the twin themes of Mark, spiritual baptism and spiritual food, by first explaining the nature of spiritual meaning in Mark.

" . . . saying one thing and signifying something other than what is said is called allegory."
Pseudo-Heraclitus

CHAPTER IV

SPIRITUAL MEANING IN MARK:
All Things in Parables

Literal Interpretation and the Function of Allegory

Because most scholars in the nineteenth century considered Mark a literal historical report that was derived from Peter, they focused on the gospel's simplicity of style and "realistic" portrayal and ignored signs that pointed to a spiritual or allegorical interpretation. Of course, Mark interpreted the Parable of the Sower as an allegory and presented the Parable of the Vineyard as a transparent allegory. If Mark found a deeper meaning in Jesus' parables, did he also find a deeper meaning in the stories he told about Jesus? There is, for example, an indication that the stories of Jesus feeding the two multitudes had a deeper meaning, which the disciples misunderstood just as they had previously misunderstood the parables. Jesus attempted to lead the disciples to an understanding of the feeding stories just as he had explained to them the Parable of the Sower before. There is a difference between allegorizing a text in which a literal meaning was intended and interpreting allegorically a text in which a deeper meaning was intended; the former is illegitimate, but the latter is not. After we discuss literal meaning, and the function of allegory, we will explain Mark's allegorical interpretation of the Parable of the Sower. The allegorical or spiritual interpretation always held negative implications for the literal meaning of the text. While the spirit elevated, enlivened, and inspired faith, the letter downgraded, deceived, and destroyed faith. According to Paul, " . . . the letter killeth, but the spirit giveth life." (II Cor. 3:6). The early Church fathers emphasized the sublime nature of the allegorical interpretation; they did not dwell on the objectionable character of the literal meaning. This task was left to their Jewish and pagan opponents, who used the literal story of the Bible against Christianity, to which the church fathers responded with the allegorical interpretation. Origen even agreed that the Bible, taken literally, contained many absurd, contradictory, and fictional elements, which were designed to point one to their higher meaning. Origen wrote,

> "Consequently the divine wisdom has arranged for certain stumbling blocks and interruptions of the historical sense to be found therein by inserting in the midst a number of impossibilities and incongruities, in order that the very interruption of the narrative might as it were present a barrier to the reader and lead him to refuse to proceed along the pathway of the ordinary meaning: and so, by shutting us out and debarring us from that, might recall us to the beginning of another way, and might thereby bring us, through the entrance of a narrow footpath, to a higher and loftier road and lay open the immense breadth of the divine wisdom."[88]

The church fathers encased the Bible in a thick allegorical coating, which protected it until the literal story broke through again in late medieval and early modern times.[89] The allegorical method was a victim of its own success. After the complete victory of Christianity over its Jewish and pagan opponents, there appeared to be no longer a need for the allegorical defense of the literal story. At the same time during the Middle Ages civilization sank to the level at which the barbarisms of the Old Testament history no longer presented such a stark contrast to the events that one encountered in every day life. It seemed only natural to view medieval history as a continuation of the biblical story. With no opponents in sight and no incongruence felt between one's own experience and the biblical story, scholars thought it was safe to once again pay attention to the literal meaning of the story. At this point the contradictions and absurdities of the allegorical interpretations were more apparent than those of the literal story. Even Martin Luther pitted the single sense of scripture against the multiple meanings of allegory.[90]

With the progress of civilization and the enhancement of ethical consciousness during the Enlightenment came the criticism of the literal meaning of the Bible by the Deists, which was primarily a moral rather than a rational criticism. They made much of the immoralities perpetrated by such biblical heroes as Moses and David. Their rational, in contrast to their moral, criticism of the Bible was merely designed to demonstrate the inferiority of a written revelation to a natural revelation. They based this ethical critique on their high moral conception of God. This was especially true of Matthew Tindal,[91] but was best expressed by Thomas Paine.

> "It is a duty incumbent on every true Deist, that he vindicate the moral justice of God against the calumnies of the Bible.'[92]

Deists attacked the two main proofs of Christianity, which the Church used from ancient times, namely, miracles and prophecies. Thomas Woolston and Anthony Collins showed how the literal meaning of the story undermined both of these supports, and both writers recommended the allegorical interpretation as the only way to salvage the text. Woolston even appealed to Origen to back up his use of the allegorical method, but, unlike Origen, Woolston dwelt at length on the absurdities of the literal meaning of the miracles of Jesus.[93] Collins exposed the irrelevance of the Old Testament prophecies, literally understood, for their supposed fulfilling events in the New Testament. However, Collins was the more cautious of the two. He knew that the literal story, like the Gorgon who could only be looked at safely in a mirror, could only be securely viewed as it was reflected in the allegorical meaning.[94]

Both appealed to Jewish interpreters for the literal story. Woolston even quoted a perhaps fictional Jewish Rabbi throughout his discourses. Collins referred to a work by Surenhusius, in which the author claimed to have learned about early Jewish methods of interpretation from a converted Rabbi. These methods, which, Surenhusius argued, were common to Jews and Christians, enabled him to reconcile Old Testament prophecies with their New Testament fulfilling events. Meanwhile, most Jews never "strayed" from the literal meaning of the Old Testament prophecies, so often preserved an unbroken tradition as to their literal meaning from ancient times. Even some medieval Christian scholars, such as Hugh of St. Victor and Andrew of St., Victor, who were interested in the literal meaning of scripture, also resorted to Jews to help them understand the literal meaning of the texts.[95]

However, it was one thing for Jews and pagans to use the literal meaning of the Old Testament prophecies or miracles to expose the Christian distortion of them, and quite another for Christian gentlemen, themselves, to impose the literal meaning on a believing church. Such actions did not go unnoticed or unpunished: Collins fled to Europe to escape the consequences of his actions, and Woolston went to prison and died there.

Collins, who concentrated on the prophecies, may have been on slightly safer grounds than Woolston, who attacked the miracles. After all, the church had a problem with prophecy from the beginning. The Early Catholic Church was established in opposition to prophetic groups, such as the Montanists and Gnostics. Joachim of Fiori raised the issue again in the Middle Ages, and some elements of the Reformation placed an emphasis on prophecy. The church was more reluctant to give up miracles, because, unlike prophecy, which offered salvation in the future, they offered benefits in the present.

During the Enlightenment theologians were busy providing religion with a rational basis. Whereas previously miracles were a proof of God's presence, in the Age of Reason the orderly course of nature became the principal argument for the existence of God, the argument from design. These two arguments were diametrically opposed to one another: the one saw God in the orderly course of nature and the other experienced the divine in the irregular interruptions of that order, miracles. As the laws of nature became more firmly established, instead of being proofs of God's action, miracles, themselves, needed to be proven. This was the point of Hume's criticism. He raised not the question of the possibility of miracles, but that of the evidence required to prove them. Actually, since his philosophy presumed no necessary or logical connection between the cause and the effect, but only a customary or conventional expectation that the one followed the other, it allowed for the possibility of miracles. What he denied was that it was possible to prove that a miracle had actually taken place—even if it had. It would always be more likely, he argued, that the story of a miracle was the product of human credulity than that a miracle had in fact occurred.[96]

Finally, the strongest point made by both Collins and Woolston was that the allegorical interpretation is found in the New Testament, itself. As long as they confined themselves to recognizing allegory in the New Testament, they were on the right track. After all, no one could object to interpreting allegorically a text that was allegorical in character. Scholars agreed that Mark interpreted the Parable of the Sower as an allegory. If, as some persuasively argue, this parable were a model for understanding Mark's gospel, then most of the gospel must be interpreted allegorically. When Jesus' disciples asked him about the Parable of the Sower, he said "Do you not understand this Parable? How then will you understand all parables?"(Mk. 4:13). As we pointed out earlier, "this parable" stood for the individual story and "all parables" the gospel story as a whole.

Even before Julicher, the development of the historical critical method was the story of a struggle to establish the single grammatical meaning of the text to replace the four levels of meaning of the medieval allegorists: literal, analogical, tropological, and spiritual.[97] Origen had recognized three levels, the literal, moral, and spiritual, based on his tripartite anthropology, in which man consisted of a body, soul, and spirit. In practice Origen fused together the last two levels, moral and spiritual, under the influence of a more fundamental dualism of matter and spirit.[98] Modern literary critics have taught us that once we admit that a text has multiple meanings, we have no way to decide how many levels of meaning are acceptable. Avant garde literary critics recognize virtually endless layers of meaning in narrative, which is tantamount to denying that a story has a determinant meaning.

The Parable of the Sower

It is necessary to distinguish between recognizing allegorical texts, and allegorizing non-allegorical ones, and to permit multiple levels of meaning only where more than one level of meaning is intended and signaled by the text. The Parable of the Sower is a good place to begin, since it has been widely recognized that Mark interpreted the Parable allegorically. After the Parable and its interpretation a further application to the surrounding narrative appears to be called for. Therefore, the gospel of Mark contemplated four different versions of the Parable: (1.) the Parable, itself, (2.) its interpretation, (3.) its application to the characters in Mark's story, (4.) and its appropriation by the hearers / readers of the gospel. The vicissitudes to which the Parable was subjected in subsequent history was probably not in Mark's purview. In his flight from Mark's allegorical interpretation Jeremias emphasized the Parable's realistic character.[99] However, John Drury maintained that Jeremias found all the realistic description not in the Parable, itself, but drew it from his knowledge of or assumptions about Palestinian agriculture. According to Drury,

> "Mark does not tell us that the sower 'comes striding over the stubble,' (Jeremias's words) nor that the path had been 'trodden over the stubble' by the 'villagers,' nor that the sower sows there 'intentionally,' nor above all that he intends to plow in."[100]

All this realistic description Jeremias read into the Parable. Moreover, Drury argued that a parable by its very nature was anything but realistic. It frequently utilized fantastic and unnatural imagery, which was valued for its symbolic meaning and not for its realistic portrayal.

Jeremias defined realistic in terms of ancient farming technology with its supposed practice of sowing before ploughing.[101] However, the divergence between ancient and modern conceptions of agriculture was not just a matter of different levels of technological achievement and practice. The problem was that the ancients had an entirely different view of "nature" than ours, one which could hardly be described as realistic. It was precisely this primitive view of sowing that made it such an appropriate image of death and resurrection.

Witness the ease with which the gospel of John introduced a saying from Mark about death and resurrection (or eternal life) with the figure of sowing.

> "Truly, truly, I say to you unless a grain of wheat falls into the earth and dies, it remains alone; but if it dies, it bears much fruit. He who loves his life loses it, and he who hates his life in this world will keep it for eternal life." (Jn. 12:24-25 and Mk. 8:35).

Paul also used sowing as an image of death and resurrection.

> "You foolish man! What you sow does not come to life unless it dies. And what you sow is not the body which is to be, but a bare kernel, perhaps of wheat or of some other grain. But God gives it a body as he has chosen, and to each kind of seed its own body." (I Cor. 15:37-38).

In other words the ancient farmer believed that when a seed was planted in the ground, it died. In order for it to grow into a plant a miracle was required; divine intervention was needed—"But God gives it a body." While on the microscopic level we have to do with the death and resurrection of the seed, on the macroscopic scale we have to do with the seasonal death and resurrection of vegetation. In the nature religions the apparent death of vegetation in winter and its resurrection in spring was associated with the death and resurrection of the gods—Baal, Osiris etc. Paul cast the Christian God in a similar role in relation to the seed.

In a small but provocative book entitled, *Who Do People Say I Am?* Marvin W. Meyer described this primitive view of nature.

> "Often the emergence of fertility upon the face of the earth—the growth of crops, the birth of babies, the rebirth of the year—was pictured as the fruition of cosmic intercourse between the sky god and the earth goddess. The rain, or semen of heaven, penetrates into the womb of the earth,

> impregnating the earth with life itself. Such life is the gift of the divine Father, the rider of clouds, who goes by names like Zeus, Jupiter, El, and Baal."[102] And Yahweh!

So when the ancients read or heard the Parable of the Sower, they may already have thought of death and resurrection before they heard the interpretation. They may have already been predisposed to think of the mystery of the kingdom of God and the "word" (λόγος) with reference to death and resurrection once Jesus introduced these terms. This brings the Parable of the Sower into line with the death and resurrection language elsewhere in Mark.

When we, like John Drury, interpret the parables in the context of the gospel narrative, we must keep in mind that neither the meaning of the individual parable nor that of the gospel story as a whole is a known quantity at first. As we interpret the individual story or parable, we have simultaneously to reformulate the overarching story. The resurrection theme that we find in the healing stories is not supported by the usual view of Mark with its almost exclusive emphasis on the suffering theme. However, the notion of resurrection entered Mark's story as early as that of suffering. Every time that Jesus predicted his death, he also foretold his resurrection. As we have seen, through the idea of sowing, the teaching about death and resurrection permeated the Parable of the Sower as well.

The sower was not identified in the interpretation of the parable. The only individual named in the interpretation was Satan (the birds). The rest of the interpretation dealt with various groups and the way they received and responded to the word: the ones along the path, on rocky ground, among thorns, and on good earth. Mark did not use the Greek word for seed in the parable, but always referred to it pronominally. In the interpretation Mark referred to the seed no less than seven times as the word (λόγος).

It was only when Mark applied the Parable to the characters in the gospel that he identified individuals instead of groups, and defined what the word (λόγος) meant. The sower was Jesus, the Son of Man, who sowed the word (λόγος) by speaking it plainly when he predicted his death and resurrection in Jerusalem (Mk. 8:32). Satan, who was identified as the birds in the interpretation of the Parable, immediately stole the message from Peter (Mk. 8:33) just after Jesus sowed it. The rocky ground of the parable may also refer to Peter, the rock.

John Drury called attention to the use of the term word (λόγος) in the story fulfilling or illustrating the third group in the parable, the seed sown among thorns. They are described as " . . . those who hear the word, but the cares of the world and the delight in riches, and the desire for other things, enter in and choke the word and it proves unfruitful." (Mk. 4:18ff.). When the rich young man was told to give away his possessions to the poor and follow Jesus, who was on his way to the cross, Mark said that the man refused, " . . . on account of the word (λόγος)." ("επί τω λόγω"). (Mk. 10:22)[103]

However, Drury stopped short of a complete interpretation of the Parable when he denied that there was a narrative fulfillment of the prophecy about the good soil and its abundant crop. He claimed that no one in the story reached " . . . that happy condition."[104] This oversight is understandable since literary critics have referred to the persons, who represented the good soil as "The Little People."[105] It was "For this word (λόγος) . . ." (διά τουτον τόν λόγον) that the Syro-Phoenician Woman's request was granted (Mk. 7:29), and it was the "word" that the deaf man heard (understood) clearly (Mk. 7). Not only did the Syro-Phoenician woman illustrate the good soil, but also provided the key to the feeding stories that preceded and followed her own.

As important as it is, sowing is not the principal image for death and resurrection in Mark; the main symbol came, not from agriculture, but from the early Christian ritual of baptism.

Mark A Gospel In Two Parts

The two-part structure, which is found in the parable and its interpretation, is also exhibited in the overall structure of the gospel of Mark. It is derived from the parabolic or allegorical nature of the gospel, which requires a story and its interpretation. This twofold structure of Mark has not gone unnoticed. Both historical and literary critics have agreed that Mark naturally divides into two parts, which correspond to two successive locations of Jesus ministry: Galilee and Jerusalem. Scholars also noticed that Jesus worked different miracles in the two parts of the gospel. In the first half of Mark Jesus performed healings that granted health and life, which represented death and resurrection; in the second half of the gospel he gave sight to the blind and speech to the mute, which represented the understanding and expression of the word (λόγος) concerning Jesus' death and resurrection. While the historical critic maintained that Mark's account fell into two parts because that was the way things happened, the literary critic argued that the gospel divided into two parts because that was the way Mark told Jesus' story.

Historical and literary critics appeared to agree on the turning-point in Mark's narrative: Peter's confession at Caesarea Philippi. However, a closer look reveals a subtle shift in the precise point that separated the two parts of Mark: the historical critic chose as the turning point in the gospel what he believed to be a historical event, Peter's Confession; in contrast the literary critic selected a comment of the gospel author, "He said all this quite openly"(Mk. 8:32). This comment may have been anticipated in Mark's comment at Jesus' healing of the deaf mute, "And he spoke plainly."(Mk. 7:35).

Historical critics considered this change to plain speech a shift from a hesitant to a bold manner of speech on Jesus' part; literary critics regarded it as a change from an obscure to a clear form of speech, which corresponded to the parable and its interpretation. For the literary critic this change marked not just a difference in the way Jesus spoke, but an alteration in the way Mark told Jesus' story. It is significant that the misunderstanding theme followed both the parables (Mk. 4:10 and 13), and the scene at Caesarea Philippi (Mk. 8:32-3).

Mark's comment about Jesus' speaking plainly followed Jesus' first clear prediction of his death and resurrection. However, the comment applied to the entire second half of the gospel, because what followed was nothing but a repetition and elaboration of the first prediction of Jesus' passion. Although the comment about speaking openly did not accompany the second (Mk. 9:30) and third (Mk. 10:33-34) predictions of the passion, it must have been presupposed as the latter two predictions were almost identical with the first one. The comment also applied to the story of Jesus' death and resurrection, which fulfilled the predictions. Therefore, Mark's comment about Jesus' speaking openly separated the parabolic telling of the gospel story from its interpretive retelling.

It was generally agreed that the parables of Jesus in Mark were tales told twice: once in parabolic or obscure form and again in interpreted or plain form. Mark's comment after Jesus' first prediction of his death and resurrection, "He said all this quite openly.", could also have accompanied the interpretations of the parables. Since the publication of William Wrede's *Messianic Secret* in 1901[106], it has come to be widely recognized that Mark's story of Jesus also had a veiled, secret, or parabolic character, which, like the parables, required an interpretive retelling. Not only the stories Jesus told, but also the stories Mark told about Jesus were parables. Although Mark gave an interpretive restatement of the Parable of the Sower, it has been generally assumed that he failed to give a similar interpretive retelling of the gospel story as a whole. However, we will maintain that Mark gave an interpretive retelling not just of the individual parables, but of the entire gospel story. In the interpretive retelling John the Baptist and Jesus became Elijah and the Son of Man.

Like the Parable of the Sower, Mark told the story of John the Baptist twice: once using the name John (Mk. 1:4-15), and again using the name Elijah (Mk. 9:12-13). When he told the story of John's preaching and baptizing, Mark never called him Elijah, but the description fit that prophet.

> John: "... and had a leather girdle about his waist..."
> (Mk. 1:6)
> Elijah: "... with a girdle of leather about his loins."
> (II Kings 1:8)[107]

Mark also used the name John in the account of the Baptist's death (Mk. 6:17-29).

It was only when Mark reflected on the significance of the Baptist's death that he called him Elijah. The interpretive retelling of the Baptist's story occurred in a dialogue between Jesus and three of his disciples (Peter, James, and John) as they descended the mountain after Jesus' transfiguration.

> "And they asked him, 'Why do the scribes say that first Elijah must come'? And he said to them 'Elijah does come first to restore all things; and how is it written of the Son of Man that he should suffer many things and be treated with contempt? But I tell you that Elijah has come and they did to him whatever they pleased, as it is written of him.'" (Mk. 9:11-13).

The name John did not occur in this passage; only Matthew made the identification of John with Elijah explicit (Matt.

17:13). In the retelling of the Baptist's story Mark used the name Elijah, but what he said happened to Elijah fit John the Baptist. Unlike Matthew, Mark nowhere clearly said that John the Baptist was Elijah; the identification has to be inferred from the way Mark told the story.

Mark also told the story of Jesus twice: once using the name Jesus (Mk. 1:1-8:30), and again adding the title Son of Man (Mk. 8:31-16:8). When Mark wrote about Jesus in the first half of the gospel, he attributed to him such miracles as to suggest that he was divine, but the title Son of Man occurred only twice (Mk. 2:10, 28). Conversely, when Mark wrote about the Son of Man in the second half of the gospel (Mk. 8:31, 38; 9:9, 12, 31; 10:33, 45; 13:26; 14:21, 41, 62), he told the story of Jesus' death and resurrection in Jerusalem. When Mark used the name Jesus, the description fit the Son of Man, and when he added the title Son of Man, the description fit Jesus. Nowhere did Mark unequivocally state that Jesus was the Son of Man. Again, it was Matthew who made the identification explicit.

> Mark: "Who do men say I am?" (Mk. 8:27)
> Matthew: "Who do men say that the Son of Man is?" (Matt. 16:13).

Further evidence that the story was told twice is provided by the repetition of the introductory elements in the narrative. The prophecy introduced the first telling of the story of John and Jesus (Mk. 1:2-4). An allusion to the same prophecy introduced the interpretive retelling of the story (Mk. 9:11-13). Mark defined the beginning of the gospel in terms of something Isaiah wrote, and referred to it with the phrase, "As it is written in Isaiah the Prophet." (Mk. 1:2). When Mark used the same quotation formula to introduce the story of Elijah and the Son of Man, it is clear that we are back at the beginning of the gospel. Therefore, when Mark spoke about the death of Elijah "... as it is written of him." (Mk. 9:13), and the death of the Son of Man "... how it is written of the Son of Man, that he should suffer many things ..." (Mk. 9:12), he was referring back to the messenger prophecy (Mk. 1:2-4). It was the only prophecy in Mark that referred both to John the Baptist and Jesus.

If Mark told the story of John and Jesus twice, then there should be some kind of correspondence between the first and second half of the gospel. If we consider Jesus' journey to be baptized by John as introductory, then Jesus first preached in Galilee after which he went to Jerusalem to die. However, when we include all of Jesus' movements reported in Mark, we bring to light an unexpected parallelism between the two halves of the gospel. In the first half of Mark, Jesus went to Judea to be baptized by John; after John was arrested, Jesus returned to Galilee (Mk. 1:14). The pattern was repeated in the second half of Mark: Jesus / Son of Man went to Jerusalem to be crucified; he promised his disciples that, after his resurrection, he would go back to Galilee to meet them there.[108]

There is even evidence to suggest a correspondence between what happened in Judea and Galilee in the two parts of the gospel. Since for Mark death and resurrection and baptism were symbolically interchangeable (Mk. 10:38), the account of Jesus' journey to be baptized could be taken as a symbolic account of his death, and resurrection. His return to Galilee in the first half of Mark culminated in his transfiguration, which has been connected with either his resurrection or parousia. In the second half of Mark Jesus referred to his anticipated death in Jerusalem as his baptism (Mk. 10:38). Jesus promised his disciples that after his resurrection, he would return to Galilee where they would see him. This seeing, like that at the transfiguration, has been referred to both the resurrection and the parousia. The parallelism of the two parts can be illustrated graphically.

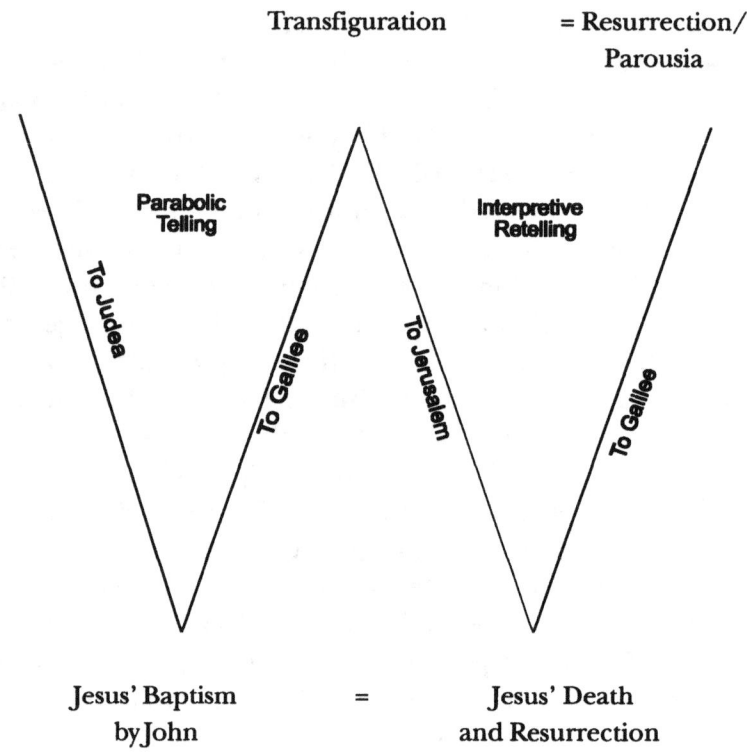

From the preceding illustration one can see that the various sections of Mark are disproportionate. The brevity of the story of Jesus' journey to be baptized by John in the parabolic account (Mk. 1:9-11) is compensated for by the detailed report of the Son of Man's trip to be crucified in Jerusalem in the realistic account (Mk. 8:31-15:47). The reverse is true of Jesus return to Galilee: it is detailed in the parabolic recounting (Mk. 1:14-9:8), and brief in the interpretive retelling (Mk. 16:1-8). The reason for this is simple: Jesus' death was a past event, the story of which could be told realistically in detail, but his return to Galilee and post-resurrection appearance to his disciples was a future event, which could only be told in detail in parabolic form. So the entire story was told in detail only once: half in realistic form—Jesus' / Son of Man's journey to death—and half in symbolic form—Jesus' / Son of Man's journey back to Galilee after he was baptized by John.

As with all allegories, the two stories can be reduced to one story—first told in symbolic form and then retold in realistic or interpreted form. At this point our graphic illustration should be revised.

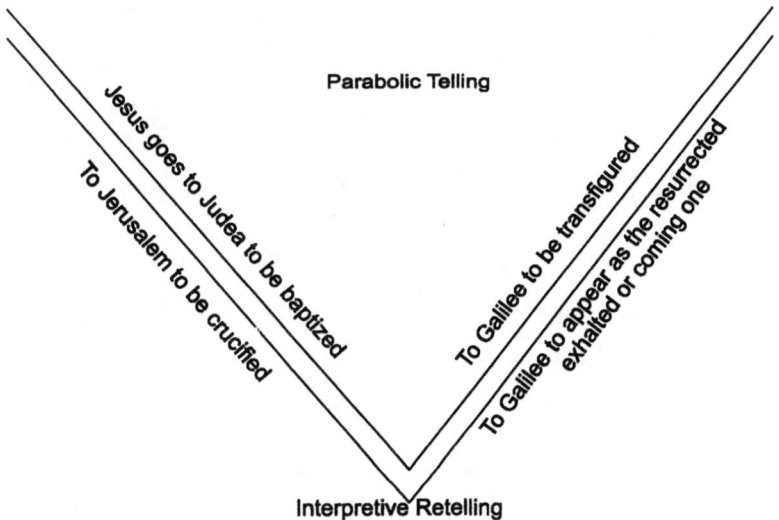

In other words Mark's Jesus went to Judea only once to be baptized (crucified), and returned to Galilee only once to be transfigured (or appear as the risen / coming one).

"I have baptized you with water;
but he will baptize you with the Holy Spirit."
(Mk. 1:8)

CHAPTER V

SPIRITUAL BAPTISM IN MARK:
Dying and Rising

Corresponding to the two levels of meaning in Mark, the literal and the spiritual are two types of baptism: John's water baptism and Jesus' spiritual baptism. According to Mark Jesus' spirit baptism followed and replaced John's water baptism, and Jesus' ministry only began after John was arrested (Mk. 1: 14). Mark nowhere indicated that Jesus' disciples were baptized with water, because they were called by Jesus after John's baptism had ceased. Noticing this "omission," the other gospel authors indicated that some of Jesus' disciples were first disciples of John the Baptist (Jn. 1: 40 f.f). However, that does not appear to have been Mark's view. Scholars have failed to find many references to baptism in Mark because they were looking for water baptism instead of spirit baptism. If we accept Mark's definition of spirit baptism as martyrdom or death and resurrection, we discover that baptism is one of the main themes of Mark.

The Problem of Baptism in the Gospels

From a historical point of view, Schweitzer called attention to the non sequitur in regard to water baptism in the gospels. He wrote,

> "Why did Jesus continue the preaching of the Baptist and not also his baptism? That this question should

never have been thought worthy of investigation will always appear unintelligible."[109]

Water baptism stopped with the ministry of John the Baptist and started again spontaneously in the early church. The gospel of John attempted to make good this oversight by having Jesus' disciples baptize (Jn. 3: 22, 26; 4: 1-3), but the synoptic gospels knew nothing about this. Schweitzer ingeniously suggested that baptism was unnecessary during Jesus' public ministry because of the sacramental nature of Jesus' presence as the future messiah. If that were true, there would have been no need for any sacraments during Jesus' ministry, but Schweitzer, himself, on the very next page described the feeding of the multitude as a sacrament.[110] Therefore, Schweitzer's view did not adequately account for the absence of water baptism during Jesus' ministry.

According to Mark water baptism came to an end with John the Baptist, because Jesus' Spirit baptism replaced it. Concerning the stronger one, who would come after him, John the Baptist said,

> "I have baptized you with water; but he (Jesus) will baptize you with the Holy Spirit." (Mk.1:8)

John predicted that Jesus, when he came, would baptize with the Holy Spirit, but very few scholars claim that this prophecy was fulfilled during Jesus' ministry. The usual view is that the outpouring of the Holy Spirit on the day of Pentecost (Acts 2) fulfilled this prophecy. However, that story is told in Acts, which was not even written when Mark composed his gospel. The scene in Acts also occurred after Jesus' ascension, so he could not have been the Spirit baptizer. Yet John's prophecy specifically designated Jesus the agent of Spirit baptism. Therefore, it is very unlikely that Mark had the Pentecost story in mind.

The alternative was to consider Jesus' ministry as portrayed in Mark a series of Spirit baptisms. This was probably overlooked because Jesus' ministry was one of preaching, healing, and exorcising and appeared to have nothing to do with baptism. As James M. Robinson so aptly put it,

> "This preparatory significance of John's baptism is stressed (v.8) by stating the relationship and contrast between the ministries of John and Jesus in terms of two kinds of baptism. For apart from this interest in placing John's baptism in a correct relationship to Jesus, it is not customary for Mark to present Jesus' activity from the point of view of a kind of baptism he administered."[111]

Why did Robinson bother to deny that Mark portrayed Jesus' ministry in terms of the type of baptism he administered if that notion were not implicit in John's prophecy? If the obvious meaning of the prophecy had not pointed to Spirit baptism in Jesus' ministry, Robinson would not even have considered that alternative, as his explicit rejection of that interpretation showed that he did. Robinson appears to be saying that if we understood John's prophecy in a straight forward manner, we would expect Mark to have portrayed Jesus' ministry as a series of Spirit baptisms. Instead, Robinson claimed that Mark confined himself to contrasting the ministries of John and Jesus in terms of the two kinds of baptism that they administered. However, if John baptized with water, and Jesus did not baptize with the Holy Spirit, there was no contrast. There was simply an unfulfilled prophecy.

Apparently, Robinson looked for a fulfillment of the prophecy in Mark, because in a footnote to the passage in which Jesus described the martyrdom of James and John as baptism (Mk. 10: 38–39), Robinson observed,

> "10:38-29 and 1:8 are not parallel in meaning for Mark, although they could have been for John and Jesus."[112]

Robinson recognized that these two passages belonged together. If Mark 10: 38-39 and 1: 8 were parallel in meaning for Mark, then Jesus' ministry could be understood as a series of Spirit baptisms. Robinson, himself, hinted at such a possibility when he referred to

" . . . the baptism of Jesus by the Spirit (v.10) . . ."[113]

If the descent of the Spirit upon Jesus at his baptism by John could be called a baptism by the Spirit, then the exorcisms, in which the unclean spirits were driven out of a person and the Holy Spirit came in, should also be characterized as Spirit baptism.

Robinson's suggestion that for John and Jesus the two passages (Mk. 10: 38-39 and 1: 8) could have been parallel in meaning implied that the ministry of the historical Jesus could have consisted of a series of Spirit baptisms. Robinson denied that the two passages were parallel in meaning for Mark. However, agreement between the prophecy and its fulfillment was more likely in the gospel of Mark than in the ministries of John and Jesus. After all, John could have predicted that Jesus would baptize with the Holy Spirit, and Jesus could have conducted his ministry along entirely different lines. Since he had control of the story, but not of the history, Mark could have conformed the fulfilling events to the prophecy and that was exactly what he did.

We now have a book on the Spirit in Mark, which was written by M. Robert Mansfield, a professor at Oral Roberts University in Tulsa, Oklahoma. Since its founder, Oral Roberts, was a Pentecostal minister, the university is known for its emphasis on the Spirit. In his preface Mansfield wrote, "Focus on the presence, power, and gifts of the Holy Spirit is indigenous to the purpose and ethos of the university."[114] He entitled his work *Spirit and Gospel in Mark*, but did not locate Jesus' Spirit baptism in Mark. Instead, like Luke, Mansfield placed the Spirit baptism, which was announced by John the Baptist (Mk. 1: 8), in the period after Jesus' resurrection. Although he denied that Mark agreed with Luke that the Pentecost event (Acts 2) fulfilled John's prophecy, Mansfield maintained "... that Mark considers baptism with the Spirit to belong in a general manner to the period after the resurrection."[115] As he continued, Mansfield became more specific and located the fulfillment of John's prophecy (Mk. 1: 8) at a resurrection appearance of Jesus at which he baptized his disciples with the Holy Spirit.[116] It is obvious that Mansfield has not improved upon Luke's solution to the problem because there was no resurrection appearance in Mark, at which this Spirit baptism could have taken place.

Spirit Baptism in Luke: The Promise of the Father

Before one can understand Mark's view of Spirit baptism, one must dispose of a formidable obstacle, Luke's interpretation of John's prophecy (Mk. 1: 8), which has sometimes shaped the scholarly understanding of the passage. Luke had a parallel to Mark 1: 8 (Lk. 3: 16), but did not develop the implications of its location at the beginning of his gospel. Luke converted the prophecy of John the Baptist to the "promise of the father," (Lk. 24:49) which *was* fulfilled in Acts 2. The Spirit was promised and sent by the Father, and the person was baptized.

That the Spirit baptism contemplated by Mark was to have taken place during Jesus' ministry and not after his ascension, as Luke would have it, was indicated by John's designation of Jesus as the baptizer. Jesus would presumably have to have been present to have baptized with the Holy Spirit. When Luke placed Spirit baptism after Jesus' departure, he no longer considered Jesus the agent by which it was accomplished. When Luke paraphrased John's prophecy (Mk. 1: 8; Acts 1: 4-5), he shifted to the passive voice to avoid mentioning the baptizer; in Mark's version of the prophecy Jesus was the Spirit baptizer.

Although Luke did not understand Jesus' ministry as a series of Spirit baptisms, he did consider the apostles' ministry in Acts as a succession of Spirit baptisms. Luke's transfer of Spirit baptism from Jesus' ministry to the post resurrection period was part of a larger reordering of the Markan narrative in accordance with his stated intention to set the story straight (Lk. 1: 1). Prophecies that Mark apparently left unfulfilled, Luke simply transferred to Acts: Spirit baptism (Mk. 1: 8), inspired speech (Mk. 13: 11), persecution (Mk. 13: 9), and the proclamation of the gospel to all nations (Mk. 13: 10). Mark appeared to have failed to reconstitute the Twelve disciples after the defection of Judas, so Luke made good his "omission" (Acts 1: 15-26). However, Mark did not exclude Judas from the instruction to the *disciples* and Peter to go to Galilee after Jesus' resurrection.

That Luke did not consider John's prophecy as fulfilled in Jesus' ministry is shown by his repetition of it at the beginning of Acts.

> "And while staying with them he (Jesus) charged them not to depart from Jerusalem, but to wait for the promise of the father which he said, 'You heard from me, for John baptized with water, but before many days you shall be baptized with the Holy Spirit'" (Acts 1: 4-5).

The changes occasioned by Luke's relocation of John's prophecy were much more extensive and subtle than is at first apparent. "The promise of the father" no doubt referred to the promise that Jesus alluded to at the end of Luke (Lk. 24: 49). However, Luke did not simply repeat John's prophecy at the beginning of Acts, but also interpreted it. He changed the prophecy from the active to the passive voice, which dropped the mention of the Spirit baptizer, Jesus. According to Luke, Jesus, who had already ascended, could not have been the Spirit baptizer. The phrase "promise of the father" might indicate that Luke considered God the Spirit baptizer. The use of the passive voice is consistent with the hesitation to attribute activity such as baptizing directly to God. In fact the Spirit was sometimes viewed as an intermediate being, who conducted God's business in the world.

By adding the phrase, "before many days," to John's prophecy, Luke changed its temporal reference. According to Luke there was a considerable gap between John's prophecy and its fulfillment. The phrase, "before many days," obviously referred to the gap between Jesus' repetition of John's prophecy and its fulfillment in Acts (Acts 1: 4-5; 2: 1-4). Because Luke added the phrase to a paraphrase of John's prophecy, its temporal reference is ambiguous. By the phrase Luke meant "before many days" after Jesus was speaking to his disciples after his resurrection, but, added to John's prophecy, it could also have meant "before many days" after John baptized with water, which was its original meaning in Mark.

That no considerable time lapse between the prophecy and its fulfillment was contemplated by Mark was shown by the necessity which Luke felt to repeat the prophecy at the beginning of the work in which it was fulfilled. His repetition of the prophecy was a sound literary judgment. Its position in Acts (Acts 1: 4-5) is analogous to its position in Mark (Mk. 1: 8): in both cases the prophecy was placed at the beginning of the work in which it was represented as fulfilled. By repeating the prophecy at the beginning of Acts, the author tacitly recognized that its fulfillment should take place in the work at the beginning of which it appeared "before many days" and not after a long delay.

The prophecy occurred a second time in Acts in Peter's report to Jerusalem about how the gentiles received the Holy Spirit.

> "As I began to speak, the Holy Spirit fell on them just as on us at the beginning. And I remembered the word of the Lord, how he said, 'John baptized

with water, but you shall be baptized with the Holy
Spirit.'" (Acts 11: 15-16).

Note the use of the passive voice again. It is remarkable how the author of Acts has transformed a prophecy of John the Baptist into "... the word of the Lord..."!—a fact noted by Haenchen.[117]

Spirit Baptism in Mark: Dying and Rising

If the appearance of John's prophecy at the beginning of Acts signaled that the age of Spirit baptism was about to begin, then the appearance of the same prophecy at the beginning of Mark indicated that Spirit baptism began in Jesus' ministry. Mark quoted John the Baptist as saying,

> "I have baptized you with water; but he will baptize
> you with the Holy Spirit." (Mk. 1: 8).

The passage appears to imply that John's water baptism has come to an end to be followed by Jesus' Spirit baptism. John had no successor except Jesus, who baptized with the Holy Spirit and not with water. There is no hint of a long delay between the two baptisms. After John was delivered up, Jesus came into Galilee to preach the gospel. (Mk. 1: 14).

Having disposed of Luke's postponement of Spirit baptism until Pentecost, it is necessary to look for the fulfillment of John's prophecy in Mark. The way has already been prepared in an article by H. A. Blair entitled "Spirit-Baptism in St. Mark's Gospel." Although he failed to develop the implications of it, his statement of the problem cannot be improved upon.

> "Too often this promise that Christ would baptize
> with the Holy Spirit has been associated with
> Pentecost. But Mark gives no account of Pentecost;

> nor does he, like John, make clear and open reference to it in his gospel. Unless, then, he is a very poor story teller (which he is not), there must surely be a fulfillment of the promise in his gospel. If, in the story of Cinderella, her god mother had promised fairy coach, gown and slippers, and the rest of the story had contained no reference to her receiving anything of the kind, we should not be satisfied by a later editor's note explaining that the promise was fulfilled in another story: we should read the story carefully to see whether she did in fact receive something which was a symbolic fulfillment: perhaps it was not intended to be taken literally. In St. Mark, then, we are looking for a fulfillment and interpretation by Jesus of John the Baptist's prediction of Spirit baptism. Dr. Farrer suggests that the fulfillment is the healing miracles (p. 45 ff.)" [118]

Blair correctly attributed the necessity of looking in Mark for the promised Spirit baptisms to the requirements of storytelling; then he abruptly canceled this observation by discovering the Spirit baptisms in the historical order of events where no such necessity existed. In a historical account it is not necessary for a prophecy to be fulfilled; it is a literary work that sets up certain plot expectations, whose fulfillment is required by the logic of narrative. Therefore, it is more likely that Mark invented both the prophecy and its fulfillment than that the historical Jesus fulfilled expectations set up for him by John the Baptist.

We have come full circle back to the problem that caused Robinson to allocate the promise-fulfillment to the historical order of events: Mark did not appear to deal explicitly with baptism all that much. However, to find few references to baptism in Mark is to ignore his appended qualification "with the Holy Spirit," which signaled a spiritual or symbolical interpretation of baptism. Direct references to baptism were not always needed. Such an interpretation could manage with allusions to the elements of the baptismal ritual: the changing of garments, nude baptism, and its symbolic representation of death and resurrection. However, Mark also used the term "baptism," and even defined it.

When James and John asked to sit on Jesus' right and left when he reigned in glory, Jesus replied,

> "You do not know what you are asking. Are you able to drink the cup that I drink or to be *baptized* with the *baptism* with which I am *baptized*? And they said to him, 'We are able.' And Jesus said to them, 'The cup that I drink you will drink; and the *baptism* with which I am *baptized*, you will be *baptized* . . . '" (Mk. 10:38-39)

This is usually taken to be a prophecy of Jesus' death and the martyrdom of his two disciples, but it is also a definition of Spirit baptism. When Mark called the anticipated deaths of Jesus, James, and John their baptisms, he was not speaking metaphorically, but spiritually (we would say symbolically). The emphasis on baptism in this passage is unmistakable: the word for baptism is repeated in it six times, and the baptism of which it speaks is the baptism with the Holy Spirit that was predicted by John the Baptist (Mk. 1: 8). The above definition has two levels of meaning: on the one level what happens to Jesus, James, and John is called baptism, but on another level it is understood as their death. If Mark here referred to death as baptism, he elsewhere referred to baptism as death and resurrection.

Jesus Baptizes with the Holy Spirit in Galilee

After his baptism by John the Baptist, which symbolically represented his death and resurrection, Jesus returned to

Galilee as the risen Lord. Through his healing ministry there, Jesus demonstrated the resurrection powers that were at work in him. Having defined Spirit baptism as death and resurrection, Mark represented it in his narrative by allusions to the water baptismal ritual and the direct use of death and resurrection language. In the baptismal ritual the discarding of the old garment (body) represented death and the putting on of the new garment symbolized the resurrected body. In some healing stories Mark referred to the changing of garments; in others he used direct death and resurrection language. By referring to Jesus' healings as death and resurrections, Mark was also calling them Spirit baptisms.

Although Mark did not say that Jesus changed garments, when John baptized him, he did refer to Jesus' powerful radiant robe in order to suggest that he was the risen Son of Man. Jesus' shining robe at the Transfiguration represented both his baptismal garments and his resurrected body. The voice from heaven saying, "Thou art my beloved Son . . ." (Mk. 1: 11; 9: 7), which occurred both at Jesus' baptism and his Transfiguration, bound the two scenes together. Nor did Jesus' magic robe appear for the first time at the Transfiguration; earlier in the gospel a woman was healed by touching his garment (Mk. 5: 25-34). In that scene Jesus perceived that power had gone forth from him even though she had only touched his clothes. The skeptical disciples wondered how Jesus could distinguish her touch from that of others in the crowd. That he could, showed that his was no ordinary robe, but was his life giving resurrection body. Resurrection was also the theme of the framing story, the raising of Jairus' daughter (Mk. 5: 21-24, and 35-43). Mark further indicated that wherever Jesus went the sick touched the fringe of his garment and were made well (Mk. 6: 56). He even reported a rumor that miraculous powers were at work in Jesus because he was John the Baptist risen from the dead (Mk. 6: 14). Although Mark did not consider Jesus John the Baptist, the assumption that miraculous powers were at work in Jesus because he was risen from the dead was not questioned.

If Jesus' robe referred to both his baptismal garment and his resurrected body, it is likely that other references to clothing in Mark had a similar symbolic significance. Of particular interest are the stories in which a changing of garments takes place. Before the demoniac of Gadara met Jesus, he wandered among the tombs, which were obvious symbols of death. After Jesus cast the legion of demons out of him, the man was seated (like the young man at Jesus' tomb, Mk. 16: 6), clothed (was he previously naked like the young man in the garden of Gethsemane? Mk. 14: 52), and in his right mind. To demonstrate the completeness of the cure, it was perhaps appropriate to refer to the fact the demoniac was seated and in his right mind, but why call attention to the ordinary fact that he was clothed? (Mk. 5: 2-20). To anticipate our explanation, the reference to clothing would make sense if it were intended to be an allusion to nude baptism and death and resurrection.

When Jesus passed by, the blind man at Jericho threw his clothes off. In an article about this story entitled "Mark 10: 50: Why Mention the Garment?" Alan Culpepper presented a comparable view, but refused to extend it to other similar stories in Mark.[119]

When Jesus entered Jerusalem, the multitude threw their clothes on the ground and on the colt that Jesus rode. A possible commentary on this story is found in a saying in the Gospel of Thomas. Jesus' disciples asked him,

> "When will we see you?
> He answered,
> When you tread on your garments,
> And are not ashamed."

Jonathan Z. Smith considered this saying an allusion to nude baptism. The saying in Thomas has three things in common with the story in Mark: in both the people discard their clothes, tread on them, and see Jesus.[120]

Finally, the young man (νεανισκος) in the garden of Gethsemane gave up his garment at Jesus' arrest, and reappeared in a new robe at Jesus' empty tomb. According to Scroggs and Groff this story alluded to nude baptism and death and resurrection.[121] That this story framed the crucifixion scene, in which Jesus twice changed garments (Mk. 15: 17-20), tends to confirm their view.

John Drury called attention to Mark's use of "clothes as an image of change," not just any change, but the fundamental change brought about by the gospel of Jesus Christ. On the historical plane, it was a change from Judaism (the old garment) to Christianity (the new patch Mk. 2: 21 ff.); on the personal level, it was a change brought about by baptism, which involved a change of garments, which represented death and resurrection. We miss Mark's symbolism probably because we no longer think of salvation in such final terms as death and resurrection. Such a notion belonged to the apocalyptic world view that looked forward to the end of the world, while we think more in terms of transformations that enable us to live more effectively in this world. Nor do we any longer think in terms of a single conversion from a sinner to a saint, but of a number of transitions from birth to death.

Since Mark defined Spirit baptism as death and resurrection, it is only natural for him to refer more directly to these themes. Some of the miracle stories, which have no references to clothing, contained death and resurrection language: the raising of Jarius' daughter and the epileptic boy, for example. Jarius told Jesus that his daughter was "at the point of death" (Mk. 5: 23). After the interpolated story of the woman who was healed by touching Jesus' garment (Mk. 5: 24-34), some came from Jarius' house and reported, "Your daughter is dead." (Mk. 5: 35). Although Jesus denied that she was dead (Mk. 5: 39), Mark described her healing in resurrection language, "Taking her by the hand Jesus said to her 'Talitha cumi': which means, 'Little girl, I say to you, arise', and immediately the girl got up and walked, for she was twelve years old" (Mk. 5: 41, 42). Similarly after Jesus performed an exorcism on him, Mark said that the "epileptic" boy was "like a corpse"; so that most of them said, 'He is dead.' But Jesus took him by the hand and lifted him up and he arose." (Mk. 9: 26-27).

Somewhat less obvious cases of death and resurrection symbolism are the healing of Peter's mother-in-law and the paralytic. Peter's mother-in-law was lying down (like a corpse) with a fever. As he did with Jarius' daughter and the "epileptic" boy, Jesus "came and took her by the hand and lifted her up" (Mk. 1: 31). Before Jesus healed the paralytic, he was lying down (like a corpse). Jesus said the same thing to the paralytic that he said to Jarius' daughter, "I say to you, 'arise'" (Mk. 2: 11-12).

In other words Jesus was able to raise people from the dead because of his own symbolic resurrection at his baptism by John the Baptist. The healings and exorcisms, which were symbolic deaths and resurrections, were the Spirit baptisms foretold by John the Baptist (Mk. 1: 8). The symbolic or parabolic section of the gospel ended with Jesus' first prediction of his death and resurrection.

Other Baptismal Imagery in Mark

Many scholars have compared Jesus' feeding of the multitudes in the desert to God's feeding of the Israelites in the Exodus story. It is more difficult to find anyone who compared Jesus' crossing the Sea of Galilee to the Israelites' crossing the Red Sea, and yet they are logical corollaries. If Jesus' feeding the multitudes represented a eucharistic celebration, his crossing the sea with his disciples represented their baptism. It can be shown that in Mark's day the Israelites' sea crossing and desert feeding represented baptism and the eucharist. Paul, a contemporary of Mark, wrote,

> "I want you to know brethren that our fathers were all under the cloud, and all passed through the sea, and all were baptized into Moses in the cloud, and in the sea, and all ate the same supernatural food and all drank the same supernatural drink. For they drank from the supernatural Rock which was Christ. Nevertheless with most of them God was not pleased; for they were overthrown in the wilderness." (I Cor. 10: 1-5).

Just as the eucharistic interpretation depends on a connection between the feeding stories in Mark, the Lord's Supper and the Old Testament desert feeding stories, the baptismal view hinges on a relationship between the sea crossing stories in Mark, baptism and the Old Testament Exodus sea crossing stories.

In his search for a parallel to the sea miracle in Mark Bultmann overlooked the greatest sea miracles in the Old Testament, the crossing of the Red Sea and the Jordan river. Instead he looked for a sea miracle done by a Jewish child.[122] But the miracle in Mark, like those in the Exodus story, were done by the "Lord." After Jesus stilled the storm, the disciples asked, "Who then is this that even the wind and the sea obey him?" (Mk. 4: 41). The answer, which was understood in Mark and was made explicit by Matthew (Matt. 8: 25), was the Lord.

Bultmann may have been misled by the form of the story in Mark, which was that of the stilling of a storm. The prose version of the Exodus story contained no storm; the wind was simply the agent by which the Lord caused the sea to be blown back.

> "Then Moses stretched out his hand over the sea. The Lord drove the sea back by a strong east wind all night and turned the sea into dry land; and the waves were divided;" (Ex. 14:21)

However, the Psalmist's poetic version of the story did contain a storm.

> "When the waters saw you, O God,
>   when the waters saw you, they
>   were afraid;
>   the very deep trembled.
> The clouds poured out water;
>   the skies thundered;
>   your arrows flashed on every
>   side.
> The crash of your thunder was in
>   the whirlwind;
>   your lightnings lit up the
>   world;
>   the earth trembled and shook.
> Your way was through the sea,
>   Your path, through the mighty
>   waters;
>   yet your footprints were
>   unseen.
> You led your people like a flock
>   by the hand of Moses and
>   Aaron." Ps. 77:16-20
> "He rebuked the Red Sea, and it
>   became dry;
>   he led them through the deep
>   as through a desert." Ps. 106:9.
> "he made the storm be still,
>   and the waves of the sea were
>   hushed." Ps. 107:29.

Poetic license permitted the direct appearance of the Lord on the scene, which left no positive role for the wind. If the Lord were present, the wind was unnecessary and became an obstacle. Mark's account corresponds to the Psalmist's in many respects: the presence of the Lord, the wind as an obstacle, and the rebuke of the sea/wind by the Lord (Jesus). The element of fear is also present in both versions: in the Psalm the waters were afraid, and in Mark the disciples. By the time mark wrote, the poetic opposition of the Psalmist's version had issued into a dualistic struggle between the Lord (Jesus) and the demonic storm.

If we can trust Taylor, there was also something unusual about the way Mark described the action of the cloud at Jesus' transfiguration: Mark said that it covered Jesus and his disciples (Mk. 9: 7). This may correspond to Paul's statement, "Our fathers were all under the cloud ... and all were baptized into Moses in the cloud and in the sea ..." (I Cor. 10:1 ff.).

"Take; this is my body."
(Mk. 14:22)

CHAPTER VI

SPIRITUAL FOOD IN MARK:
The Broken Bread and the Broken Body of the Son of Man

When prophecy was used to prove the truth of Christianity, in the words of John Drury " . . . it drained the past, in which a prophecy was made, of real and independent meaning by channeling the prophecy so exhaustively into the present."[123] If the prophecy were a mere type or shadow of the fulfilling event, the question naturally arises, why would one bother to retain the former after the latter arrived? The answer may be found in the counter tendency of Christianity, as a new religion, to seek roots in the past lest it spring up and wither because it had no depth. In order to avoid the charge of being an upstart religion, Christianity claimed to be the true heir of the vineyard (Israel), and anchored itself in ancient prophecies. Hence, the gospel of Jesus Christ began, not with the career of John the Baptist, but with something Isaiah, the prophet wrote (Mk. 1:1-3).

In antiquity nationality and religion were so closely connected, that one was expected to acquire one's religion by being born into it. The notion that religion was a birth right was so powerful that conversion to another religion was called a rebirth. If people entered their ancestral religion by being born into it, then they entered their new religion by being "born again" into it. The background of this emphasis on rebirth in the gospel of John, and conversion in the book of Acts was the intermingling of religions in the

Greco-Roman period that gave the potential convert a number of choices.

Any new rituals or ceremonies had to be back-dated in order to give them the prestige of antiquity and the connection with an already established religion. To avoid embarrassment at the non-mention in the scriptures of the two principal ceremonies of early Christianity—baptism and the Lord's Supper—Paul proceeded to read them into the Exodus story.

> "I want you to know brethren, that our fathers were all under the cloud and all passed through the sea, and all were baptized into Moses in the cloud and in the sea, and all ate the same supernatural food and all drank the same supernatural drink. For they drank from the supernatural Rock which followed them, and the Rock was Christ. Nevertheless with most of them God was not pleased; for they were overthrown in the wilderness." (I Cor. 10:1-5).

Paul interpreted Israel's sea-crossing as their baptism, and their desert feeding as their eucharist.

It has not gone unnoticed that the two feeding stories in Mark contained eucharistic motifs. The obsolete historical version of the theory was presented by Albert Schweitzer, who pointed to the parallel expressions in the feeding stories and the Last Supper account: The giving of thanks, and the breaking and distribution of the bread.[124] Boobyer claimed that the evidence was not sufficient to prove the theory, because these elements were a part of any common Jewish meal.[125] But he failed to explain why Mark paid so much attention to the ordinary meals in a narrative that was occupied by other matters. Quentin Quesnell presented a much more convincing argument for the eucharistic interpretation without the now defunct assumption that Mark's narrative was historical.[126] Having found baptismal symbolism throughout the story, we should expect eucharistic symbolism to be equally extensive. After John baptized Jesus, the latter was in the desert for forty days, and angels ministered to him—fed him. After Jesus healed Peter's mother-in-law, she ministered to all—fed them; and after Jesus raised Jarius' daughter, he asked them to give her something to eat.

The Feeding of the Multitudes: Miracles or Parables

The only thing that stands in the way of the symbolic interpretation of the feeding stories is the assumption that they are miracle stories. If Mark had considered the desert feedings miracle stories, then he probably would have emphasized the difficulty of feeding such a great multitude with such a small amount of food. And that is usually taken to be his point. However, in Mark the problem was not that the supply of food was insufficient, but that it was a desert place. It is obvious to us that five loaves and two fishes are not enough to feed 5,000, and seven loaves and a few fishes 4,000 but no one in Mark raised that objection. Once the number of loaves and fishes was ascertained, the disciples did not question whether it were enough to feed the multitudes.

The objection in question was, of course, raised by the secondary versions of the stories: Matthew had the disciples say, "we have only" (Matt. 14:17), Luke, "No more than" (Lk. 9:13), and John, "but what are they among so many?" (Jn. 6:9). These early interpreters of Mark agreed unanimously that the initial supply of food was not enough to feed the multitudes only because they read Mark's numbers quantitatively instead of symbolically as they were intended by Mark.

The notion of parable cannot be limited to the stories told by Jesus and designated as such, but must also be extended to the stories that Mark told about Jesus. Already, at the turn of the century, Wrede suggested that the stories told about Jesus in the gospel of John also had a deeper meaning and should be interpreted as parables. Then he cautiously pointed out that this may have been true of Mark as well. About John he wrote,

> "It is striking that not merely sayings of Jesus but also events in the story of his career, such as the entry into Jerusalem in 12:16 or the feet washing in 13:7, remain obscure to the disciples in their higher significance. In a certain sense this is indeed also the case already in Mark."[127]

Nineham was even more emphatic. He wrote, "The miracles of Jesus, he (Mark) thinks, have a meaning no less than the parables, and to those who understand that meaning they are 'signs' enough."[128] Mark's comment about the parables also supports this view. He did not say that for outsiders all things were spoken in parables, but rather "take place" in parables (Mk. 4:11). If the healing and exorcisms represented spiritual baptisms, then the desert feedings represented spiritual eucharists.

It is clear that the feeding stories had a deeper meaning, which required an interpretive retelling, because of the comments of Mark and Jesus following the two stories. After the feeding of the 5,000, Jesus came walking on the sea. Mark said that the disciples were astonished, "... because they had not understood about the loaves." (Mk. 6:52). This is the first clue that the stories had a deeper meaning. The need for an interpretive retelling was even more clearly indicated after the feeding of the 4,000. Subsequently, the disciples in the boat were complaining because they had only one loaf. Again, Jesus indicated that they had failed to understand the feeding stories. After the first feeding, Mark called attention to the loaves; after the second feeding, Jesus singled out the leftovers.

The Loaves and the Leftovers

According to Mark, Jesus fed two different multitudes, but the stories are so similar that some scholars have suggested that we have to do with a doublet. There are at least three possibilities: either Jesus fed two different multitudes and both accounts are historical, or he fed one multitude and the two accounts represent different reports of the same feeding, or both accounts are fictional. Since the baptismal and eucharistic symbolism requires only one sea crossing and one feeding in the desert, it becomes necessary to explain the doublet. The framework of the Parable of the Vineyard must be kept in mind: in the Parable the beloved Son's death opened up salvation to the gentiles. It was this overarching Jew / gentile theme that demanded two sea crossings and two desert feedings: the first multitude fed was Jewish, the second gentile, and the broken bread the broken body of the beloved Son.

Robert Fowler rejected the identification of the first multitude with the Jews and the second with the gentiles, which obviated the necessity for two stories. His first reason for rejecting the view in question was that it was just a variation on an ancient interpretation,[129] the implicit assumption being that if the view were ancient, it could hardly be accurate. His second reason was the supposed absence of any support for the view in the text.[130] If he had considered the Syro-Phoenician woman's story in detail, he would have found that it supported the ancient interpretation. His bare mention of the woman's story in connection with eating scenes in Mark was insufficient to reveal its true bearing on the desert feeding stories.

After Jesus questioned the disciples about the left over fragments from the two desert feedings, he asked them, "Do you not yet understand?" (Mk. 8:21). Fowler conceded that the interpreter of the gospel does not know what the disciples ought to understand.[131] Again Fowler's impasse was due to his twin failure to consider the Syro-Phoenician woman's story, and accept the ancient identification of the two multitudes as Jewish and Gentile respectively.

If the eucharistic interpretation of the feeding stories and the above identification of the two multitudes proves to be correct, what the disciples misunderstood was that the broken bread, Jesus' body, was sufficient for both Jews and gentiles. In the ensuing narrative the disciples misunderstood Jesus' predictions of his death, which he described using the broken bread at the Last Supper. Mark brought these two themes together in the Parable of the Vineyard, in which the beloved Son's death effected a transfer of the vineyard from Israel to the gentiles. Therefore, what the disciples failed to comprehend was not merely the necessity for Jesus' death, but also the opening of salvation to the gentiles that resulted from it.

Even the story of John the Baptist's death may have eucharistic overtones. We are so familiar with the details of the story and they are just consistent enough with the imagined decorum at an oriental potentate's court that they conceal how unusual the story really is. Beheading was, perhaps, common enough, but serving the severed head on a platter at a birthday banquet was a bit out of the ordinary for even a Herodian ruler. Fowler rightly recognized that the Baptist's death involved a "Last Supper" of sorts for which John's broken body provided the main course.[132] Just as John's head was on a platter ready to eat, Jesus' body was distributed to his disciples as the broken bread at the Last Supper. John's body was also "distributed" to his disciples: "When his (John's) disciples heard about it, they came and took his body, and laid it in a tomb (Mk. 6:29).

The desert location of the two feeding stories also has a symbolical significance, which connects it with the Exodus story. After crossing the Red Sea, the Israelites were fed in a desert; after being baptized by John, Jesus was fed in a desert place by angels; finally, after each of the two sea crossings in Mark, Jesus fed a multitude in a desert. The emphasis on the desert setting for the feeding of the five thousand was unmistakable: Jesus asked his disciples to accompany him to a desert place (Mk. 6:31) to rest for a while; Mark said that they then went away by boat to a desert place (Mk. 6:32); and, finally, Jesus' disciples told him that they were in a desert place (Mk. 6:35). Many have concluded that Mark was alluding to the feeding of the Israelites in the Old Testament.[133] The detailed comparison of the two has been done enough times that it need not detain us. We will discuss the symbolic elements in the feeding stories themselves.

However, the numerical allusions in the stories are so complex that it is difficult to know exactly where to begin their interpretation. Austin Farrer began with the numbers of the two multitudes: five thousand and four thousand, which, he said, leads one to expect a third multitude of three thousand.[134] But these were not the numbers in the story to which Jesus called the disciples' attention. John Drury pointed out certain clues in Jesus' discussion of the feeding with his disciples. Drury maintained that when Jesus recalled the two feeding stories, he emphasized the numbers. However, Jesus did not treat all the numbers equally as Drury seemed to imply by his summary that omitted Mark's syntax.

> "6: 35-44 5 loaves among 5,000 left 12 baskets of bits.
> 8:1-10 7 loaves among 4,000 left 7 baskets of bits."[135]

Although Drury is an undisputed master of a laconic style, here he has omitted too much, for from this simple listing one cannot determine which figures Mark considered more important: the number of loaves, the size of the crowds, or the number of the leftovers; one can determine the relative significance of these various elements only by adding Mark's syntax back to the statement and quoting it in full.

> "'And do you not remember? When I broke the five loaves for the five thousand, how many baskets full of broken pieces did you take up?' They said to him, 'Twelve.' 'And the seven for the four thousand, how many baskets full of broken pieces did you take up?' And they said to him, 'Seven.' And he said to them, 'Do you not yet understand?'" (Mk. 8:18-21).

In each case Jesus mentioned the number of loaves and the number of people fed in an introductory dependent clause, "When I broke the five loaves for the five thousand" "And the seven for the four thousand"—and the number of baskets of fragments in the main clause, "how many baskets full of broken pieces did you take up?" and "how many baskets full of broken pieces did you take up?" Jesus called attention not only to the number of baskets, twelve and seven, but also to the fact that the loaves were now in the form of fragments.

In his Socratic questioning of his disciples Jesus brought together the numbers from the two desert feeding stories, so one should bring them together in the interpretation. It has long been recognized that the numbers twelve and seven, could have represented Israel and the Gentiles respectively. When brought together, the loaves, the five of the first feeding and the seven of the second, equal twelve loaves, only enough for Israel. John Drury suggested a solution to the problem by calling attention to an earlier story in Mark in which Jesus justified the disciples gathering food to eat on the Sabbath by referring to the case of David who fed his men (Israel) with five loaves, which left seven for the Gentiles (Mk. 2:25, 26; I Sam. 21:3)[136] After Jesus, like David, fed Israel, the five thousand, with five loaves, he had seven left over for the Gentiles, the four thousand. As David gave to his men the shewbread, which was intended for the priests, Jesus gave to the gentiles bread, which was intended for Israel. In the Syro-Phoenician woman's story Jesus gave to the gentiles crumbs from the bread which was intended for the children (Israel).

One question remains. If the multitudes were filled, why was it necessary for Mark to show that there was enough left over to feed both Israel and the gentiles again, the twelve and seven baskets full? The connection with the Exodus story may provide the clue for tying up this loose end. In the wilderness the Israelites were commanded to gather only enough manna for one day. If they gathered more, it spoiled (Exo. 16:20). There was just one exception to this rule: on the day before the Sabbath they were to gather enough for the Sabbath eve and the Sabbath. In this one instance the excess manna did not spoil. (Exo. 16:24) In Mark the Sabbath was the Eschaton, of which the Son of Man was Lord (Mk. 2:27-28).

The Syro-Phoenician Woman: the Key to the Feeding Stories

The Syro-Phoenician woman's story falls between the two feeding stories, which is an example of a frequently used Markan technique, whereby he begins one story, tells a second story, and then completes the first story. The numerous links between the desert feeding stories and the Syro-Phoenician woman's story suggests that Mark intended the reader / hearer to compare them. The Greek word for "filled," εχορτάσθησαν, which was used in the feeding stories, was terminologically linked to the word for "fed," χορτασθηναι, which appeared in the woman's story.[137] The double feeding theme (five thousand / four thousand, and children / dogs) formed a second link between the two stories. Finally, both the desert feeding stories and the woman's story had left over fragments / crumbs.

The Syro-Phoenician woman's story supports the ancient identification of the first multitude fed, the five thousand, as Jewish, and the second multitude, the four thousand, as gentile. Some interpreters have identified the first or both multitudes as gentile, but that would have canceled the point of the woman's story.[138] Its dramatic development and suspense depended on the fact that only the Jews had been fed so far. If the gentiles had already been fed, Jesus' answer to the woman's request for help would never have been in doubt. The position of the woman's story between the two desert feeding stories was crucial. When the woman asked Jesus to heal her daughter, he had just fed the Jews, the five thousand. In his reply to her request, Jesus continued the bread theme from the first desert feeding story, "Let the children first be fed, for it is not right to take the children's bread and throw it to dogs." (Mk. 7:27). Although Jesus had just fed the Jews, it was by no means certain that he would also feed the gentiles. However, by saying that the children (Jews) must be fed *first*, Jesus left open the possibility that the dogs (gentiles) could be fed *second*.[139] The Syro-Phoenician woman seized upon this possibility, and picked up the fragment theme from the first desert feeding story. She said, "Yes, Lord; yet even the dogs (gentiles) under the table eat the children's crumbs." (Mk. 7:28). Her mention of the crumbs showed that she recognized that the leftovers from the feeding of the Jewish multitude were available to feed the gentile multitude.

In the Parable of the Vineyard the death of the beloved son, which was symbolized by the broken bread at the Last Supper, opened up salvation to the gentiles. The Syro-Phoenician woman understood that the broken bread, Jesus' death, made salvation available to the gentiles. By failing to comprehend Jesus' reference to the fragments the disciples failed to understand how Jesus' death brought salvation to the gentiles. Now the misunderstanding of the disciples at Caesarea Philippi follows naturally. They failed to understand Jesus' prediction of his death and resurrection because they had previously failed to understand that the fragments from the two desert feedings represented the broken body of the Son of Man.

When Jesus granted the woman's request "For this saying" ("Διά τουτον τον λόγον," Mk. 7:29), the saying (λόγος) in question was her reference to the crumbs, broken bread, which represented the death of the Son of Man. The story of the deaf mute took up this theme of understanding from the woman's story, and developed it in terms of hearing and speaking clearly. The deaf mute's speaking "clearly" anticipated Jesus' speaking the word (λόγος) "plainly" at Caesarea Philippi when he predicted his death and resurrection (Mk. 8:32). The Syro-Phoenician woman spoke the correct word immediately just as the deaf mute was healed and spoke clearly right away. This ready response provides a contrast to that of the disciples, who were preoccupied with their failure to bring enough bread, and the blind man, who, after Jesus' first attempt to heal him, still saw men like trees walking.

Men Like Trees Walking (Mk. 8:24).

When Jesus laid hands on the blind man at Bethsaida, he asked him,

> "'Do you see anything?'
> And he looked up and said 'I see men; but they look like trees, walking.'" (Mk. 8:23b-24).

Then Jesus laid hands on the man's eyes and the man,

> "... looked intently and was restored, and saw everything clearly." (MK. 8:25).

Why did the man see men like trees walking before he saw everything clearly?

In Shakespeare's Macbeth there were also walking trees. A messenger told Macbeth,

> "As I did stand my watch upon the hill, I looked toward Birnam and anon (at once) methought, The wood began to move."

Of course, the enemy had cut down trees to use for camouflage, so they could approach the castle unnoticed. The reader instantly understands the meaning of this marching forest because of something that happened earlier in the play. An apparition had told Macbeth that he,

> "shall never vanquished be until Great Birnam Wood to high Dunsinane Hill shall come against him."

In my opinion the walking trees in the gospel of Mark are subject to the same kind of explanation. Something elsewhere in the gospel should enable us to make sense of the walking trees in the story of the blind man. Mark developed two themes that run parallel in the gospel: the one had to do with hearing and not understanding; the other dealt with seeing and not perceiving. In the Parable of the Sower the two themes occurred together,

> "so that they may indeed see
>   but not perceive
> and may indeed hear
>   but not understand;"
> (Mk. 4:12)

These same two themes were repeated just before the healing of the Blind man of Bethsaida,

> "Having eyes do you not see,
> and having ears do you not hear?" (Mk. 8:18)

Mark illustrated these sayings about hearing, and seeing (understanding) by having Jesus heal a deaf mute and two blind men. Deaf men have ears, but cannot hear, and blind men have eyes, but cannot see. Seeing men like trees walking represented seeing but not understanding.

The healing of the deaf mute followed the story of the Syro-Phoenician woman's clear understanding of the first desert feeding story. The healing of the blind man of Bethsaida in two stages followed that of the disciples' misunderstanding of the two feeding stories. When Jesus granted the woman's request "For this saying (λόγος)," the saying or word in question was the one about the crumbs or broken bread. The phrase "For this saying (λόγος)" pointed forward to the comment in the story of deaf mute "And he spoke plainly," which in turn anticipated the statement that followed Jesus' first prediction of his death and resurrection, "and he said this plainly." (Mk. 8:32). What the Syro-Phoenician woman said, the deaf mute spoke clearly, the blind man saw clearly and the disciples failed to understand was the same thing about which Jesus spoke plainly, namely, the death and resurrection of the Son of Man.

Mark contrasted the correct response of the Syro-Phoenician woman and the clear speech of the deaf mute, after Jesus healed him, with the dullness of the disciples and the partial blindness of the man who saw men like trees walking. The woman spoke the word about the children's bread leaving crumbs for the dogs. She understood that if the bread were broken (Jesus died), there would be enough for both Jews and gentiles. After the feeding of the second multitude, the disciples were still struggling with this problem

> "Now they had forgotten to bring bread; and they had only one loaf with them in the boat. And he cautioned them, saying, 'Take heed, beware of the leaven of the Pharisees and the leaven of Herod.

> And they discussed it with one another, saying, 'We have no bread.' And being aware of it, Jesus said to them, 'Why do you discuss the fact that you have no bread?'" (Mk. 8: 14-17).

In this boat scene the bread symbolism continued. The one loaf, which is not broken, is Jesus. The loaf is not broken because Jesus has not died. It will be broken at the Last Supper at which time Jesus will explain to them that it is his body. The Syro-Phoenician woman understood that when the bread was broken (when Jesus died), there would be enough bread for both Jews and gentiles. Since Peter rejected the notion of the Son of Man dying, he cannot understand the broken bread as the body of Jesus. When Jesus called attention to the twelve and seven baskets of fragments he was saying, "This is my body, which is broken."

Even after Jesus' explanation, the disciples apparently still did not fully understand. Like the blind man in the very next story they saw men like trees walking. To the disciples Jesus had said, "Having eyes do you not see;" to the blind man he said, "Do you see anything?" The disciples and the blind man were expected to see or understand that the fragments represented the broken body of the Son of Man. Like the blind man, who saw men like trees walking before he saw clearly, Peter recognized that Jesus was the Christ, but rejected his death. That the blind man was finally healed and saw clearly suggests that Peter will come to understand Jesus' sufferings.

Jesus' prediction of his death and resurrection was a culmination of the themes of the broken bread and the word (λόγος), which was first spoken in a parable by the Syro-Phoenician woman, spoken clearly by the deaf mute, and then plainly by Jesus himself. It is astonishing that the Syro-Phoenician woman was one of the first to speak the word! The final explanation of the broken bread theme came at the Last Supper.

> "And as they were eating, he took bread, and blessed, and broke it, and gave it to them and said, 'Take; this is my body.'" (Mk. 14:22).

At the Last Supper Jesus gave the broken bread to the Twelve as he had earlier given the broken bread to be distributed to the multitudes. The broken bread was a parable, a symbolic representation of the death of Jesus, which would bring salvation to both Jews and gentiles.

The focus on the theme of understanding in Mark may also clarify the motives for Jesus' silencings. Perhaps he does not permit the people and demons to speak because they do not have a proper understanding of the word. The Gerasene demoniac, who was "in his right mind," was not silenced. Instead he was told to, "Go home to your friends, and tell them how much the Lord has done for you, and what mercy he has shown you." (Mk. 5:19). Nor was the Syro-Phoenician woman silenced. Because of her saying about the dogs eating the crumbs under the table, her child was healed. Nor were the disciples silenced indefinitely, but only until after the resurrection of the Son of Man. Then Jesus told them to " . . . say whatever is given you at that time, for it is not you who speak, but the Holy Spirit." (Mk. 13:11). Jesus' silencings may also be conditioned by the requirements of the Markan plot.

"Sprechen ist silbern,
Schweigen is gelden—

Speech is silver,
Silence is golden."

CHAPTER VII

SILENCE IS GOLDEN:
The Motives of Jesus' Silencings in Mark

Literary criticism has made possible a unique solution to the problem of the messianic secret in Mark in terms of plot requirements. Aristotle spoke of a character's reversal of fortune brought about by a discovery of who or what that character represented.[140] Discovery is also called recognition as when Peter at Caesarea Philippi recognized that Jesus was the Christ, or when the Jewish leaders discovered who Jesus claimed to be. However, different consequences flowed from these two recognition scenes: Peter's confession was followed by the first prediction of Jesus' death and the Jewish leaders recognition of Jesus' claims was followed by their issuance of a death sentence against him. It has been noticed that each of Jesus' predictions of his death was followed by misunderstanding by the disciples and Jesus' teaching on discipleship and suffering.[141] Without Jesus' teaching on suffering the disciples' recognition was incomplete. That was also the point of Jesus' healings of a deaf mute and two blind men, which represented the opening of their understanding, and what they understood was the necessity for Jesus' sufferings.

Both the timing and the meaning of the messianic recognition was different for Jesus' followers than it was for his enemies. The disciples' misunderstanding led to Jesus teaching them and presumably to eventual better understanding. With Jesus' enemies there was no question of their understanding or believing in him. When they recognized him, they condemned him to death. In this regard the plot of the Parable of the Vineyard and the Gospel of Mark are identical. The silencings then served a dual purpose: To allow time for the disciples to receive the teaching about Jesus' suffering, and to delay the recognition of Jesus by his enemies to prevent his premature death.

It may be that the title, which Peter used in his confession, the Messiah, was considered inadequate by Jesus because it failed to include the element of suffering, which Jesus associated with the title Son of Man. However, Jesus called attention to quite a different problem with the title, Messiah. For Mark's Hellenistic audience (Jew or gentile) it was not enough to say that Jesus was the messiah. There was a further question, "Whose son is he?" (Mk. 12:35-37). In Mark's view messiah was a designation that required a further specification as to lineage. For some Jews the answer to this question was simple: the messiah was the son of David. However, to Mark's Hellenistic audience this seemed inadequate. In that context the culturally accepted way to honor an exceptional person—philosopher, emperor, or Messiah—was to consider him a god or a son of god.[142] Roman republicans and conservative Jewish monotheists, rejected this solution, but Mark's Hellenistic audience (Jew or gentile) proclaimed the Roman Emperor a god and the Jewish Messiah the Son of God!

Not only were Peter and the disciples silenced by Jesus, but also the demons and the people who were healed. Having inferred the messianic secret from Jesus' silencings, scholars debated whether to attribute the secrecy theme to Jesus or to Mark. In other words did Jesus, from prudential or other considerations, keep his messiahship a secret (John Locke and Albert Schweitzer), or did Mark use the secrecy theme to introduce the messiahship into a non-messianic tradition about Jesus (Wrede)? Both sides started with the silencings from which they inferred the messianic secret. We will instead begin with the more fundamental themes of recognition / non-recognition, and understanding / misunder-standing, which may reveal more clearly the motives for Jesus' silencings.

Not only were the silencings connected with the recognition and understanding themes, but were also related to a whole series of ideas, which Mark presented in pairs: silencing and ordering to speak (Demoniac—Go tell!), muteness and speaking, deafness and hearing, and blindness and seeing, which were metaphorical allusions to ignorance and understanding. The blind men were those who had eyes to see, but did not perceive; the deaf-mute was one who had ears to hear and a tongue to speak, but did not understand or speak clearly. On the way to Caesarea Philippi Peter showed that he was mute in this sense. In contrast to Jesus, who spoke clearly about his death and resurrection, Peter rejected Jesus' sufferings, which demonstrated that he understood the things of men and not the things of God.

Because one is expected to take thought before speaking, logically we should consider the understanding before we deal with speaking and silencing. There are two circumstances that prevent the present day reader from noticing how pervasive the understanding theme is in Mark. The first has to do with Mark's location of thinking in the heart. An expression such as "hardness of heart" does not refer to a lack of feeling, but to a lack of understanding. After science localized thinking in the brain, the heart came to be used as a symbol of the emotional life. The second thing that concealed Mark's references to the understanding was his use of the senses to illustrate the presence or lack of understanding. Jesus' healing of blindness and deafness referred not to the curing of the senses, but to the healing of the understanding.

To further complicate matters Mark wrote about two levels of knowledge: recognition and understanding, which corresponded to the parable and its interpretation. The higher level of knowledge, which was reserved for insiders, was the full understanding of the mystery of the kingdom. This type of knowledge was promised to Jesus' disciples, but was also possessed by certain other persons in Mark, such as the Syro-Phoenician woman and the Centurion at the cross, both of whom were gentiles. The object of this deeper understanding was an awareness of the necessity for Jesus' suffering. Anyone who lacked this type of knowledge had to be silenced to prevent the wrong message from spreading among believers. The primary object of the lower level of knowledge, which even the demons and Jesus' opponents were capable of possessing, was the recognition of Jesus' identity as the beloved Son of God. Anyone who knew who Jesus claimed to be had to be silenced to prevent Jesus' identity from becoming known to the authorities too soon, lest Jesus come to an untimely end. When the tenants in the Parable of the Vineyard recognized the beloved son, they killed him and claimed the vineyard as their own. Similarly, once the authorities learned that Jesus claimed to be the Son of God, they condemned him to death. The understanding theme, which was directed to insiders, was developed in the Parable of the Sower; the recognition theme, which was aimed at outsiders, was developed in the Parable of the Vineyard.

Silence and Understanding in Mark: The Parable of the Sower

When Jesus silenced the demons, disciples and people who were healed, he may have been saying to them, "Silence is golden. You do not understand enough to make a proper confession." Certainly, the demons did not fully understand him. They knew that he was the Son of God (recognition), but did not comprehend the necessity for his suffering and death (understanding). Peter knew that Jesus was the Christ (recognition), but, under Satan's influence, rejected the notion of his suffering, which showed that he understood the things of man and not the things of God. Finally, the people who were healed were unable to make an adequate confession until they were made whole, not only in their bodies, but also in their understanding, which was symbolized by the healings of the deaf mute and two blind men.

The Parable of the Sower was framed by references to hearing, which stood for perceptive hearing or understanding. Jesus introduced the Parable with the word, "Listen," and ended it with the saying, "Let anyone with ears to hear listen!" (Mk. 4:3 and 9). Jesus said that for outsiders "everything comes in parables; in order that 'they may indeed listen, but not understand; so that they may not turn again and be forgiven.'" (Mk. 4:11-12). He said something similar when the disciples misunderstood the feeding stories, "Do you have eyes, and fail to see? Do you have ears, and fail to hear?" (Mk. 8:18).

Before he interpreted the Parable of the Sower, Jesus challenged his disciples to understand this parable so that they will understand all parables. "Do you not understand this parable? Then how will you understand all parables?" (Mk. 4:13). Four times the interpretation of the parable referred to "hearing" the word (λόγος) (Mk. 4:15, 16, 18, and 20). The first three groups heard the word, but did not understand it. The rocky soil referred to the hardened hearts (lack of understanding) of the disciples, especially Peter, whose name in Greek meant rock. When the disciples failed to understand the feeding stories, Jesus said, "Are your hearts hardened?" (Mk. 8:17). What Peter and the other disciples failed to understand was the necessity for Jesus' death and resurrection.

In contrast to the first three groups, the fourth group heard the word and understood it. What the Syro-Phoenician woman, who represented the good soil, understood was what the disciples failed to understand, namely, the necessity for the death of Jesus. The crumbs, about which she spoke, represented the broken body of the Son of Man. As Jesus died on the cross, the centurion confessed that he was, indeed, the Son of God. Unlike the demons, disciples, and people who were healed, neither the Syro-Phoenician woman nor the centurion was silenced by Jesus. They were permitted to speak because they had a correct understanding of the word (λόγος). Jesus also promised his disciples that in the future the Spirit would speak through them (Mk. 13:11).

It was only after Jesus had healed their understanding that he permitted the people to speak. Before Jesus told the Gerasene demoniac to go home and tell his friends how much the Lord had done for him, Mark said the demoniac was seated, clothed, and *in his right mind* (Mk. 5:15). The Syro-Phoenician woman spoke the word (λόγος), not clearly, but in a parable about the dogs (gentiles) eating crumbs that fell from the children's (Israel's) table. The deaf-mute's ears were healed so that he could hear and understand; his tongue was healed so that he could speak clearly. In contrast to the Syro-Phoenician woman, he spoke clearly, but Mark did not say that he spoke the word (λόγος). Jesus was the first person in Mark to both speak the word (λόγος) and to speak it clearly (Mk. 3:32). The two blind men were healed so that they could see and perceive correctly. Assuming that the first blind man, who was healed in two stages, represented the disciples, who misunderstood the feeding stories, his complete healing should have given hope to the disciples that they would eventually fully understand. When the second blind man of Jericho was healed, he showed that he understood by following Jesus on the way of suffering (Mk. 10:52).

Silence and Recognition in Mark: The Parable of the Vineyard

The second motive for Jesus' silencings in Mark had to do with the recognition theme of the plot. If the understanding theme implied that the demons, disciples, and people who were healed should not speak because they did not know enough to make a proper confession, then the recognition motif suggested that they should keep silent because they knew too much. Mark said that Jesus would not let the demons speak, because they knew who he was (recognized him), but that did not mean that they understood him. When Peter confessed that Jesus was the Christ (recognized him), the disciples were sworn to secrecy. Like the demons, Peter understood so little that he rejected Jesus' prediction of his death and resurrection. Jesus indicated that Peter was under the influence of Satan, and understood the things of man and not the things of God. (Mk. 8:33).

> What I have called "recognition" Aristotle called "discovery." "A discovery is, as the very word implies, a change from ignorance to knowledge, and thus to either love or hate, in the personages marked for good or evil fortune."[143]

The function of the recognition theme in the plot of Mark is clearly revealed in the Parable of the Vineyard. When the tenants (Jewish leaders) recognized the owner's (God's) beloved son and heir (Jesus), they killed him in order to lay claim to the vineyard. The recognition that led to consequences in terms of the plot was not the recognition by the demons, disciples, and people who were healed, but the recognition by the Jewish leaders. The injunctions to silence were not so much designed to prevent Jesus from becoming known to potential followers, but to prevent Jesus' identity from becoming known to the authorities too soon. In the Parable of the Vineyard the recognition of the beloved son occurred at the end of the story, and resulted in his death.

Mark clearly spelled out the stages by which Jesus came

to the attention of the Jewish leaders. The silence that Jesus enjoined on the others he, himself, also observed until the proper time. When the Pharisees asked for a "sign from heaven" attesting to his authority, he refused their request (Mk. 8:11-12). The "sign from heaven," which Jesus refused to give, was probably the same as the voice from heaven affirming Jesus divine sonship at his baptism and transfiguration. The miracles were not called signs from heaven by Mark. At Jesus' baptism the voice "from heaven" was for him alone. Note the direct address.

"*You* are my beloved son." (Mk. 1:11)

At the transfiguration of Jesus the voice "from heaven" was for the disciples who were present. Note the third person.

"*This* is my beloved son." (Mk. 9:7).

The authorities never heard this voice from heaven, so never got their "sign from heaven."

Again, Jesus maintained his silence when the Jewish leaders asked him by what authority he "cleansed" the Temple. They asked him,

"By what authority are you doing these things, or who gave you this authority to do them?" (Mk. 11:28).

Jesus asked them whether John's baptism were "from heaven" or of men—an allusion to the voice "from heaven" at Jesus' baptism, and Transfiguration, and the Pharisee's request for a sign "from heaven." They could not say "from heaven" or he would have asked them why they did not believe him (John). Nor could they say "of men" because they feared the people who considered John a prophet. So they told him that they could not answer. Then Jesus said that he would not tell them by what authority he was doing these things (Mk. 11:28-33). Of course, his authority came from the voice from heaven at his baptism and transfiguration.

In the Parable of the Vineyard Jesus did not reveal his identity as the beloved son of God to the Jewish leaders. They only understood that the parable was told against them, but they did not yet know that Jesus claimed to be the beloved son (Mk. 12:1-12). Later in the Temple, when Jesus raised the question as to whose son the messiah was, the Jewish leaders still did not know that Jesus claimed to be the messiah (Mk. 12: 35-37). It was only when Jesus answered in the affirmative the High Priest's question, "Are you the Messiah, the Son of the Blessed One?" (Mk. 14: 61-62), that the Jewish leaders knew who Jesus claimed to be. They immediately condemned him to death, as the tenants of the vineyard had done, when they recognized the owner's beloved son and heir of the vineyard.

Jesus' own silence as to his identity, and eventual revelation of it to the High Priest can be compared to the silence and recognition themes in the life of *Secundus the Silent Philosopher*. A story was told to explain why Secundus, a Pythagorean, observed silence religiously. The virtue of silence was demonstrated by showing what happened when Secundus spoke. He was testing the proposition, which was called a parable (παραβολή), that "every woman can be bought; the chaste one is only she who has escaped notice." To test the parable or byword he arranged to purchase his own mother as a prostitute. They slept together all night, but did not have sex. Of course, this sparked her curiosity about his identity.

> "Then she asked him who he was, and he said to her, 'I am Secundus, your son.' And she condemning herself and unable to bear the sense of shame, hanged herself. Secundus, having concluded that

it was on account of his own talking that his mother's death had come about, put a ban upon himself, resolving not to say anything the rest of his life. And he practiced silence to the day of his death."[144]

Both Secundus and Mark utilized the themes of silence and recognition. When Secundus spoke his mother learned that he was her son; as a result of this recognition, she committed suicide. When Jesus broke his initial silence, the High Priest learned that he claimed to be the Son of God; because of this discovery, the court condemned Jesus to death. The High Priest had just asked Jesus to answer the charges against him. Mark said that Jesus,

" . . . *was silent and did not answer.* Again the High Priest asked him, 'Are you the Christ, the son of the blessed one; and Jesus said, 'I am . . .'" (Mk. 14:60-61).

As soon as they learned who Jesus claimed to be, they condemned him to death.

There are, of course, some important differences between Secundus and Mark. In Secundus the breaking of the silence was done in ignorance of the consequences, which fell on his mother and not on him. Whereas in Mark the breaking of the silence by Jesus was deliberate and the consequences, which were foreseen, fell on Jesus, himself. Both Secundus and Jesus were tested by the authorities, Secundus by the Emperor Hadrian and Jesus by the Jewish authorities and Pilate. Hadrian marveled at the silence of Secundus, and Pilate at the silence of Jesus. Pilate said,

"'See how many charges they bring against you. *But Jesus made no further reply,* so that Pilate was amazed." (Mk. 15:4-5).

Finally, the mythical heroes that underlay the two stories

were different. In the case of Mark it was the Jewish notion of the Messiah and the Hellenistic concept of the Son of God. Behind Secundus was the barely disguised image of the tragic Oedipus. Many of the elements of the Oedipus story are found in the life of Secundus: his leaving home, the death of his father, his returning unrecognized by his mother (although Secundus recognized her), his sleeping with his mother (Oedipus married his mother), and the tragic consequences that followed the recognition scene. It is interesting to compare the treatment of the senses in Oedipus, Secundus, and Mark. When the tragedies struck, Oedipus blinded himself, and Secundus refused to ever speak again. In preparation for his passion Jesus healed a deaf-mute and two blind men, and broke his own silence about his identity. While Oedipus' suffering was tragic, horrific, and cathartic, Jesus' suffering was vicarious, pathetic and salvic.

"This is not the end. It is not even the beginning
of the end. But it is, perhaps,
the end of the beginning."
Sir Winston Churchill

CHAPTER VIII

NARRATIVE WORLD AND STORY WORLD:
The Two Beginnings And
Two Endings In Mark

Story and Discourse in Mark

After Mark had Jesus appoint twelve *men* to be his disciples, teach them, and send them out to proclaim the coming reign of God, he had three *women* witness one of the most crucial events in the gospel, the empty tomb. Mary Magdalene, Mary the mother of James, and Salome went to Jesus' tomb and found it empty except for a young man, who was dressed in a white robe (Mk. 16:1-8). The young man told the women that Jesus had been raised, and commanded them to "... go, tell his disciples and Peter that he is going ahead of you to Galilee; there you will see him, just as he told you." (Mk. 16:7). The women "... went out and fled from the tomb, for terror and amazement had seized them; and they said nothing to anyone, for they were afraid." (Mk. 16:8)

The women have often been faulted for not delivering the young man's message, but the real question is why they were entrusted with it in the first place. One is tempted to speculate that Mark had an enlightened preference for women in a male dominated society. Luke appears to have been critical of the role Mark assigned to the women. When the women delivered the message, Luke says, their "... words seemed to them (the male disciples) an idle tale, and they did not believe them." (Lk. 24:11). Their message had to be confirmed by a male disciple, Peter, before it was believed. (Lk. 24:12). Even in Mark the young man's message was first given to Jesus' disciples in the form of a prophecy. After the Last Supper, Jesus told his disciples, "You will all become deserters; for it is written, 'I will strike the shepherd, and the sheep will be scattered.' But after I am raised up, I will go before you to Galilee." (Mk. 14: 27, 28). To fulfill this prophecy about the scattered sheep, the disciples had fled and were presumably in hiding making it necessary for Mark to turn to the women to witness the empty tomb. However, it was the disciples, not the women, who were to see Jesus in Galilee.[145]

The protracted debate about the truncated ending of Mark is accompanied by a somewhat less prominent dispute about the equally abrupt beginning of the gospel. To ask why Mark began his narrative with the messenger prophecy and John the Baptist is to ask why he did not also include the story of Jesus birth. The answer is found in the first line of Mark in which he asserted that Jesus is the Son of God; the beloved Son of God needed no birth story, because his true family was not his earthly family, but his heavenly one.

To ask why Mark ended his narrative with the empty tomb is to ask why he did not include resurrection appearances. The answer is found in the ending of Mark's *story* in which Jesus is to return on the clouds as the Son of Man. This required Jesus to be in heaven and not on earth appearing to the disciples. Those who object to Mark's ending his gospel with the women fleeing the empty tomb speechless with fright forget that this is the end of Mark's narrative, but not he end of the story. From Seymour Chatman's *Story and Discourse* we have learned that a story has two endings: the narrative ending and the story ending. It also has two beginnings: the narrative beginning and story beginning. In Chatman's terminology the story consists of all the events referred to in a narrative arranged in absolute chronological order; the narrative or discourse is simply the order in which the story is told.[146] For example, Mark's narrative begins with the title "The beginning of the gospel of Jesus Christ, Son of God" and a prophecy from Isaiah (sic), and ends with the women fleeing the empty tomb (Mk. 1:1-3, and 16:8). However, Mark's story begins with "the beginning of creation" (Mk. 10:6, and 13:19), and ends with the coming of the Son of Man (Mk. 13:26). This can be represented graphically,

Story beginning/narrative beginning—narrative ending/ Story ending

Beginning of creation/Isaiah's prophecy—women fleeing the tomb/Coming of the Son of Man

The debate about the ending of Mark's *narrative* has diverted attention away from the ending of his *story*. While the narrative ending may leave one hanging in mid air, the story ending is completely satisfactory. In a farewell address to his disciples Jesus narrated the events leading up to the end of the story, the coming of the Son of Man. In the gnostic gospels this kind of revelation was frequently delivered by the risen Jesus.[147] However, since Mark included no resurrection appearances, he found it necessary to have Jesus convey this information about the future in a speech delivered before his death (Mk. 13). If Mark had intended to relate a resurrection appearance, as some have claimed, this farewell address would have been unnecessary.

Because Jesus' farewell address is a narrative within a narrative, one can once again distinguish between story and discourse. Like the gospel, the story of the farewell address begins with "the beginning of creation" (Mk. 13:19), and ends with the coming of the Son of Man (Mk. 13:26). But the narrative begins with the coming of false Christs, (Mk. 13:6, 7), and ends with the disciples watching and waiting for the end (Mk. 13:37). The narrative of the farewell address ends just short of the end of Mark's story world. While Mark's narrative ends with the women fleeing the empty tomb, the narrative of Jesus' farewell address ends with the disciples waiting the coming of the Son of Man.

Since the resurrection appearances fall in the period covered by Jesus' parting remarks, it is surprising that studies of Mark failed to ask what Mark's attitude toward these appearance stories was, and whether he commented on them or ruled them out by what he had Jesus say there. In fact Jesus appeared to rule out any appearance of Christ on earth prior to his coming again. He warned his disciples that many would come claiming to be the one—Ἐγώ εἰμί—the same words Jesus used in his answer to the High Priest (Mk. 13:6, and 14:62). The title Christ did not appear in this first passage. However, when he returned to the subject a little later, Jesus used the term Christ, but the emphasis shifted from the ones who claimed to be Christ to the ones who claimed to see Christ. He said that if anyone says to you, "Look! Here is the Messiah!' or 'Look! There he is!'—do not believe it." (Mk. 13:21). As an afterthought, he said, "False messiahs and false prophets will appear." By this Mark seems to be denying the resurrection appearances, themselves, because of their apparent local character. The only kind of appearance that Mark allows is the coming on the clouds preceded by cosmic signs such as the darkening of the sun and the moon and the falling of the stars. According to Mark Christ would not appear here or there privately to an individual or small groups, but on the clouds for all to see.

The counterpart to Mark's denial of local appearances of Christ before his coming on the clouds is the empty tomb story, a non-appearance story. The young man at the tomb told the women, "Do not be alarmed; you are looking for Jesus of Nazareth, who was crucified. He has been raised; he is not here. Look, there is the place they laid him." (Mk. 16:6). The statements from Jesus' farewell speech and the young man's words belong together because of the many terms they have in common. Put together they spell out a clear message: "And if anyone says to you at the time, 'Look! Here is the Messiah' or 'Look! There he is!'—do not believe it.'! (Mk. 13:21). "He has been raised; he is not here." (Mk. 16:6).

Since Mark ruled out a resurrection appearance, the appearance in Galilee could only have been a parousia appearance on the clouds of heaven. The young man at the tomb had said, "But go, tell his disciples and Peter that he is going ahead of you to Galilee, *there you will see him*, just as he told you." (Mk. 16:7). Those who claim that the phrase, "You will see him," refers to the parousia or coming on the clouds, call attention to the parallel expressions that Jesus used in his reply to the High Priest, "and you will see the Son of Man." (Mk. 14:62). However, they overlooked the parallel in Jesus' farewell address to the first word, "there." Unless the coming on the clouds (parousia) were intended, there would be a contradiction. Jesus had said, "And if anyone says to you, . . . 'Look! *There* he is!'—do not believe it." (Mk. 13:21), and the young man said, "*there* you will see him." (Mk. 16:7).

This would imply that Mark believed that Jesus was raised or translated directly to heaven at his death. As Adela Yarbro Collins has pointed out, at the time Mark wrote translation (ascension) was the culturally accepted way to indicate that a hero—whether philosopher, Caesar, or Son of God—had overcome death and was exalted and honored by God.[148] Appearances and translations were equally impressive alternative evidences that one had escaped or overcome death. However, Mark allowed Jesus, after his death, to appear only at his coming again.

When he rejected them, it is by no means certain that Mark understood the resurrection appearances, which may also have been parousia appearances originally. It was only as it became evident that the End had not happened that they came to be viewed as local occurrences, and came to be understood as resurrection appearances. In an eschatological context the resurrection of Jesus was connected with the general resurrection. Paul maintained this original connection between Jesus' resurrection and the general resurrection; he called Jesus the "first fruits" of the ones who slept (I Cor. 15:20). For Paul the appearance of Christ was not an individualistic experience, but was associated with the transformation of the whole world. Even before Paul, the appearance of Christ may have been a communal experience. The tradition that Paul received asserted that Christ had appeared to over five hundred people *at one time* (I Cor. 15:6). The gospel of Matthew may also contain a legendary attempt to keep Jesus' resurrection and the general resurrection together (Matt. 27:53). In apocalyptic, resurrection is an end time event.

The study of the resurrection of Jesus has come up with some surprising results. There is no account of his coming out of the tomb in the New Testament. Only the gospel of Peter makes good this "omission" by portraying Christ coming out of the tomb accompanied by two other figures.[149] The original appearances of Christ were not from the tomb or even on earth, but from heaven, which suggests the parousia. The same conception is presupposed by Mark's order of events: death, burial, translation and appearance from heaven. The secondary sequence is reflected in Luke's gospel and Acts: death, burial, resurrection, appearance on earth, ascension, and return. In the primary sequence the appearance followed the translation / ascension and was from heaven; in the secondary sequence the appearance was on earth and preceded the ascension. The appearance to Paul was also from heaven, but he placed it at the end of a list of traditional appearances to Peter, five hundred brethren, James and all the apostles. He did not distinguish the appearance to them from the appearance to himself. It was only later that the empty tomb story and the appearances were gradually brought together. It is ironical that Mark's empty tomb story, which was the opposite of an appearance story, became the stage scenery for the later resurrection narratives.

C. F. Evans said that something of the "seeing" of the parousia was transferred to the resurrection appearances.[150] However, no one would have transferred an event of the end time to the past when it was already known that the end had not occurred. If there were something of the "seeing" of the parousia in the resurrection appearances, it was there from the start! It is now there as a residual not a transferred constituent. What was transferred—to the future—was the parousia, itself, leaving the appearances to resemble isolated experiences of individuals. The original "resurrection" appearance may best be preserved in the vision of Christ in the Apocalypse (Rev. 1:12-16).

Early Expansions of Mark's Narrative

When a narrative isolates and organizes a segment of the story world, it plants and nourishes the seeds of its own growth. There is a natural tendency for a narrative to expand so as to encompass the entire story world. By such a process additions were made both to the beginning and ending of Mark's narrative: the birth stories and resurrection stories of Matthew and Luke. To prevent such an expansion of the narrative into the surrounding story world a gospel writer, such as Mark, would have to treat exhaustively the antecedents of all the events and characters in the narrative back to the beginning of creation and then carry the story forward to the end of time.

In one sense the entire Bible is an expansion of the gospel narrative to the limits of the story world set by Mark. Genesis represents the beginning of Mark's story world and the book of Revelation its end. This expansion of the gospel narrative may have formed one motive for the formation of the canon. If all this sounds as though too much is included in Mark's story world, just imagine the story world of a modern novel such as Carl Sagan's *Contact*, which conceivably begins with the big bang some fifteen billion years ago and ends in the singularity of a black hole at an equally remote time in the future.

The abrupt ending of Mark's narrative gave rise to several attempts to complete the gospel or continue the story in a more satisfactory manner. At least two of these efforts are connected with a comprehensive revision of Mark by Matthew and Luke. Even more remarkable, three of these attempts to improve on Mark's conclusion found their way into the text of the gospel, itself: the longer ending, which is familiar to readers of the King James Version (Mk. 16: 9-20), and two shorter endings. Some have suggested that the original ending of Mark was lost.[151]

As it stands, both ancient and modern readers have found Mark's conclusion lacking in at least two respects: (1.) the women failed to deliver the young man's message, (2.) and Jesus failed to appear to his disciples. When the modern scholar adds these two elements to the end of Mark, he does so in order to complete the narrative satisfactorily. But when the ancient reader of Mark added these elements to the end of Mark, it was with a view to continuing the gospel story.

Any explanation as to why Matthew and Luke made the changes they did must at the same time make clear why Mark ended the narrative where he did. In a word the answer is the "church," an institution that grew up since Mark. Mark mentioned the Temple and the Synagogue, but not the "church." Both Matthew and Luke had Jesus appear to the disciples so he could commission them to preach the gospel leading to the foundation of the "church." The disciples were to proclaim what Jesus did and taught (Acts 1:1), and teach them to observe Jesus' commandments (Matt. 28:20).

Nowhere in Mark did Jesus have the disciples proclaim his words and deeds; they always proclaimed the coming reign of God. Mark's proclamation was a futuristic one that pointed to the coming reign of God, not a retrospective one that looked back to the foundation of the "church" based on the words (commandments) and deeds of Jesus. Whereas Matthew incorporated the institution of the "church" in his revision of Mark (Matt. 16:18), Luke wrote the history of the beginning of the church in a separate work (Acts).

As we will soon see, it was not just the lack of a resurrection appearance in mark that bothered Mathew and Luke, but also Jesus' continued absence after his death. The absence of Jesus in Mark is related to Mark's apocalyptic stance, and is even required by it. When Mark and Mark's Jesus proclaimed the coming reign of God that meant that it was not here already, not in power at least (Mk. 9:1). When apocalyptic put the glorious reign of God and the coming of the Son of Man in the future, by the same token it removed these things from the present, which was experienced as a time of emptiness and absence. That is why Jesus was described in Mark as an absent bridegroom (Mk. 2:10-20), and absent householder (Mk. 13:34-37). A fitting motto for the gospel of Mark is the saying of the young man at the empty tomb, "He is not here." (Mk. 16:6). Jesus' absence was bearable only because Mark expected him to return soon as the Son of Man.

When the reign of God and the Son of Man did not arrive on schedule, Jesus' absence became a problem. The developing "church" required either Jesus' presence or some token of it and that is what Matthew and Luke gave it. Matthew wrote, "'... and they shall name him Emanuel,' which means, 'God with us.'" (Matt. 1:23-24).[152] Matthew also had Jesus promise "... where two or three are gathered in my name, I am there among them." (Matt. 18:20). Unlike Luke, Matthew does not have an ascension story; in its place he has Jesus promise, "I am with you always, to the end of the age." (Matt. 28:20) Since Luke does have an ascension story, he substituted the Holy Spirit for the absent Jesus.

The ending of Matthew's narrative is a consistent development of Mark's conclusion in that it has Jesus return to Galilee in accordance with the instructions of the young man at the empty tomb.

In contrast Luke's ending, which is determined by the view he developed in Acts, is not consistent with Mark's. According to Acts the disciples' mission began in Judea and moved out into the world from there.

> "But you will receive power when the Holy Spirit has come upon you; and you will be my witnesses in Jerusalem, in all Judea and Samaria, and to the ends of the earth." (Acts 1:8).

Because the mission began in Judea and not in Galilee, Luke omitted the young man's instructions to return to Galilee. In their place he put a reminder of Jesus' prediction of his death and resurrection while he was in Galilee. In Luke two men (Mark had one young man) told the women,

> "Remember how he told you, while he was still in Galilee, that the Son of Man must be handed over to sinners, and be crucified, and on the third day rise again." (Lk. 24:6, 7).

Whereas Mark and Matthew would have the disciples return to Galilee, Luke had them remain in Jerusalem. What is more important, however, is that Matthew and Luke agreed to continue Mark's story to enable his disciples to go into all the world and preach the gospel. Luke took the story one step further, and told the story of this missionary activity in Acts, making it the longest ending that was added to Mark's gospel.

Among the four gospels John's is the only one whose narrative begins at the beginning of Mark's story world, "In the beginning was the word . . ." (Jn. 1:1). Like Luke, John has the Spirit come after Jesus' ascension (Jn. 16:7) to remind the disciples of what Jesus said to them (Jn. 14:26). In John we have a more radical transformation of the gospel story. Luke's claims to accuracy, which he expressed in the conventional preface to his gospel, placed alongside John's exclusive claim to be in possession of the truth, appear to be the height of modesty. A similar exclusive claim is implied in the possibly Valentinian Gospel of Truth, whose title suggests that if it is the gospel of truth, any other gospel is false. This brings us to the question as to whether the gospels contain the gospel truth or fiction.

"I am the way, and the truth, and the life."
(Jn. 14:6).

CHAPTER IX

GOSPEL TRUTH OR GOSPEL FICTION:
One Gospel Truth and Four Gospel Stories

If Mark is fiction, is it true? Of course, it would not be true in the literal sense; otherwise it would not be called fiction. We must mean to ask: Does it contain or can it teach truth? If we say no, we not only consign the plays of Shakespeare to the realm of falsehood, but also condemn the very parables of Jesus as lies, for they were both fiction. Certainly fiction conveys truths by example, comparison, and illustration. An excellent discussion of this question of the relationship between fiction and truth is found in Alan Culpepper's *Anatomy of the Fourth Gospel*.[153]

What is the truth in fiction? It claims to know things that no one could possibly know: the unexpressed thoughts of another; to see what no one has ever seen: an unwitnessed suicide; and to be where no one has been: in another galaxy. I almost wrote on another planet, but then the claim would have been truth and not fiction, for men have been to the moon. Was the claim to have visited the moon false when it occurred in fiction (H.G. Wells' *First Men in the Moon*) before men arrived there, or did men simply get there first in their fictional imagination where many of our greatest truths originate.

Theology and literary criticism share a particularly significant term: omniscience. What to a theologian is an attribute of God, to a literary critic is a characteristic of some narrators such as Mark's. In religious fiction the omniscient

God conveys his revelation through the omniscient narrator; the implied author and narrator share in God's omniscience. In secular fiction the omniscient narrator is simply a literary device, a deliberate imaginative suspension of our human limitations adopted to facilitate the discussion of issues the consideration of which is precluded by a strict adherence to what can be known with certainty. In fiction we can know the secret thoughts of the various characters in the story; in life we are not privileged with such mind reading ability. In fiction we can tell the good guys from the bad; the villains and heroes of life are rarely as clearly distinguished as their fictional counterparts.

Problems arise when theologians take the omniscient narrator at face value and attempt to compress life into the fictional modes of the ancient gospel narratives. What Shaye J. D. Cohen said about the Jewish Torah is also true of the gospels, "A living culture cannot live in accordance with the dictates of an immovable text."[154] The gospels share these literary devices with other fictional narratives and theologians have no right to claim special exemptions from the rules that govern the interpretation of such writings. Literary criticism is applicable to both secular and religious narratives. The emphasis is usually on what is lost by such and association, but there is also a great deal to be gained. By giving up the literal truth claims for the gospels, they are free to participate in that larger quest for truth opened up by the art of fiction.

If the gospel of Mark is fiction, why has it for so long been taken to be sober history? The real reason is probably the narrative form that the gospel shares with the works of history. While fiction participates in the forms of historical narration, history exhibits some of the characteristics of fiction. Although history deals with people and events and fiction deals with characters and plots, the persons of historical narratives often assume the shape of characters and the events approximate the plots of fiction. The reverse is also true: the characters of novels are often more realistic than their historical counter parts and their stories frequently give us a glimpse into the life of a period of history that a sober historical account is ill adapted to convey. The primary difference concerns the reference not the form. History refers to events external to the report; fiction refers only to its own internal story. Literary critics speak about the "referential fallacy," that is the mistake of connecting the characters and plots of fiction with the people and events of the real world. It is the mistake people make when they enter a room where soap operas are being discussed, and think that the discussion concerns real events.

Calling the gospel of Mark, or any gospel for that matter, fiction appears to be contradictory, like calling the truth a lie. When we want to say that a thing is not to be doubted, we say that it is "the gospel truth". Fiction is story telling, and to say that one is telling a story is another way of saying that one is lying. The Valentinian gnostic did not leave the matter in doubt when he called his gospel The Gospel of Truth. In contrast the New Testament, by including four gospels naturally raised the question as to which one contained "the gospel truth". For the gospel writers themselves this was not a problem as each of them considered his gospel the only true one. Mark wrote to give expression to the oral gospel, Matthew wrote to incorporate, revise, and replace Mark, and Luke proposed to give an account that was more accurate than the many that had been written before him. Did Luke's claim to give a "more accurate" account imply that the other gospels gave a "less accurate" one? By diverging from the other three gospels more sharply (assuming that he had access to them) the gospel of John posed this question in an even more radical way. Here it was not a question of changing this or that saying or story, but of presenting an entirely different portrait of Jesus. It was early recognized that John's picture could not be harmonized with those of Matthew, Mark, and Luke. If we can believe Donald Foster, John had all the hubris of a modern historian who claims to know the past better than the people of the past knew themselves. In an article entitled: "John Come Lately: The Belated Evangelist" Foster argued that Jesus claimed for himself and John for his gospel that he was " . . . the door of the sheepfold. All who came before me (Matthew, Mark, Luke, and others) were thieves and robbers." (Jn. 10:8)[155]

Because the underlying events could only have happened in one way, we tend to weave the four gospel accounts into a single story. However, this gospel harmonizing prevents the full weight of their theologically inconvenient differences from emerging. It is ironical that scholars recognized the distinctive theologies of the narratives of the Pentateuch long before they discovered the different theologies of the four gospels. Since there was greater skepticism about the early history of Israel, there was less of a tendency to reduce the various narratives to the necessarily singular underlying course of events. In spite of the efforts of the Bright, Wright, and Albright school to shore up the Pentateuchal narratives with archaeological evidence, the critical school stemming from Wellhausen called their historical reliability into question. Besides, it was always easier for Christian scholars to see conflicts in the holy book of another religion—Judaism in this case. From the beginning the church was more critical of the "Old Testament"; it was considered only a type or shadow of the "New Testament". While the Pentateuchal narratives were fused together in the manuscripts, scholars were able to separate them in thought by recognizing their distinctive vocabulary and theological conceptions.

The reverse was true of the gospels: They were separated in the manuscripts, but were fused together in the minds of Christan scholars. For historical and doctrinal reasons New Testament theologians searched for a means of bringing the separate gospel stories together. They treated them as reliable historical reports and looked for the underlying course of events in the life of Jesus. The skepticism of Wrede and the Form Critics as to the historical reliability of the gospel narratives paved the way for a consideration of their various theological points of view. It has now become necessary to show the extent to which we are still reading the four gospel accounts as one gospel story.

If Paul preached and Mark wrote about the one gospel of Jesus Christ, how did the church end up with four gospels? The gospels were the result of the effort to produce a definitive version of the one gospel. As we have already noted, Mark wrote to replace the oral gospel preached by Paul; Matthew and Luke wrote to replace Mark. Problems arose when what was supposed to have been replaced survived. With the proliferation of gospels not only outside the New Testament, but also within it, how could one get back to the original unity of the gospel?

Actually, the notion of the original unity of the gospel was a claim put forth by Paul and Mark in the face of considerable opposition. It is clear from his letter to the Galatians that Paul did not see eye to eye with the Jerusalem community (Gal. 2:11). There was a controversy over the Jewish law and communion with the gentiles. In Paul's first letter to the Corinthians there is even evidence of a proliferation of factions.

> "For it has been reported to me by Chloe's people that there are quarrels among you, my brothers and sisters. What I mean is that each of you says, 'I belong to Paul,' or 'I belong to Apollos,' or 'I belong to Cephas,' or 'I belong to Christ.' Has Christ been divided?" (I Cor. 1:11-13).

Cephas represented the Jewish Christian community of Jerusalem. Acts claims that Apollos " . . . knew only the baptism of John." (Acts 19:25); he had not yet received the Spirit baptism. Of course, Mark subordinated John, the water baptizer, to Jesus, the Spirit baptizer (Mk. 1:8). In spite of all this original diversity, in the subsequent history of Christianity there were many attempts to recover the supposed "original unity" of the gospel.

The attempt to avert the embarrassment caused by this abundance of gospels took various forms. The choices were clear: one could, like Marcion, select one gospel (Luke), or, like Tatian, fuse the four gospels into one gospel story (the Diatesseron), or, like the church, attach a formula, "The Gospel according to . . .," that at once conceded their plurality and denied that the unity of the gospel was thereby compromised. The church asserted that there was only one gospel according to Matthew, Mark, Luke, and John.[156] It was a compromise worthy of a church that later discovered that the three persons of the trinity did not infringe on the integrity of the Godhead and the dual nature of Christ did not dissolve the unity of his person.

Irenaeus found the four gospels as natural as the four points of the compass, or the four winds, and discovered prophetic precedent in the four creatures of Ezekiel (Ez. 1:10). A similar argument to justify the multiplicity of gospels is found among the Gnostics. Following the Mosaic requirement that a thing be established by two or three witnesses (Deut. 19:15), the Gnostics chose three witnesses to the gospel: Philip, Thomas, and Matthew or Matthias.[157] The Gnostic gospels of Philip and Thomas were discovered near Nag Hammadi, Egypt in 1945. The Gnostic gospels also utilized the formula, "The Gospel according to . . ."

The author of the Muratori Canon, an early list of books approximating our New Testament, was aware of the problem posed by the four gospels. While conceding the different tendencies in the four gospels, he called attention to the one Spirit that pervaded all.

> "And therefore, though various rudiments (or tendencies?) are taught in the several gospel books,

> yet that matters nothing for the faith of believers, since by the one and guiding (original?) Spirit everything is declared in all:"

What followed was a brief outline of Jesus' career. Mentioned were his birth, passion, resurrection, interaction with his disciples, and two comings—in lowliness and in kingly power.[158]

One gospel meant one gospel story as well, so it was necessary to find a way to reduce the four gospel stories to one. In practice this meant subordinating one gospel to another, Mark to Matthew, and allowing the other two gospels, Luke and John, to supplement the story. St. Augustine called Mark an epitome of Matthew; the church agreed. When nineteenth century scholars discovered that Mark was the earliest of the four gospels, they simply subordinated the other three gospels to it. The result in both cases was one story, which the early church called the gospel and the modern church called the life of Jesus.

Although there were earlier anticipations, it was only with the development of Redaction (editorial) and literary criticism that the gospels were read as four stories instead of one. It was first necessary for scholars to form a conception of the distinctive theologies of the several gospels in order to facilitate the separation of their storylines. The separation of John from the synoptics came earlier because its chronology differed from theirs—it covered three years instead of one—and its thought and style diverged from that of the first three gospels. In his *Life of Jesus* in 1835 Strauss was able to effect the separation of John from the synoptics. However, he accepted the position of St. Augustine with regard to Mark's gospel being an epitome of Matthew's. The difficulty of overcoming the weight of a two thousand year tradition of harmonistic reading and separating the four gospel stories has not yet been fully appreciated. We still tend to read into the gospel of Mark the views of his first interpreters—Matthew, Luke, and John. We are so familiar with Jesus' story that we seldom bother to ask of each part of it which gospel writer told it that way.

It does not help that many things that were only implicit in Mark were made explicit in the other gospels. Perhaps the most prominent notion read into Mark from John was Wrede' idea of the post resurrection enlightenment of the disciples. Wrede wrote,

> "... he (John) expressly singles out the resurrection as the decisive moment in time. This Mark nowhere did in statements about the disciples. Nevertheless I have interpreted him in the light of this idea."[159]

According to Wrede, John made explicit what Mark for some reason chose to leave implicit. Connected with this idea of the post resurrection Enlightenment of the twelve disciples was John's notion that the Spirit would only come after Jesus ascended, "for if I do not go away, the helper shall not come to you" (John 16:7). It was the Spirit who was to enlighten the disciples by bringing to their remembrance what Jesus had said to them (John 14:26). Scholars have freely read this view into Mark in spite of the fact that he apparently espoused the exact opposite view. In Mark the Spirit descended like a dove upon Jesus-at his baptism (Mk. 1:10) and reascended at his death on the cross (Mk. 15:37). As the descent of the Spirit was preceded by the ripping open of the heavens (Mk. 1:10), the reascent of the Spirit was followed by the ripping open of the Temple veil from the top to the bottom (Mk. 15:37-38). If theologians were not so fearful of the gnostic view, Jesus' cry from the cross, "My God, my God, why hast thou forsaken me?' (Mk. 15:34) could be referred to this reascent of the spirit from the cross. Actually Mark does appear to countenance the "Gnostic" view, which allowed that Jesus and perhaps even the Son of Man died on the cross, but that the Spirit of God or Son of

God did not die. The gnostic view of Jesus' death is found in the Apocalypse of Peter.

> "The savior said to me, 'He whom you saw on the tree, glad and laughing, this is the living Jesus. But this one into whose hands and feet they drive the nails is his fleshly part, which is the substitute . . .'".[160]

Did Mark claim that the Spirit that descended upon Jesus at his baptism died on the cross, or that the Spirit reascended as Jesus died?

The influence of the gospel of John on our interpretation of Mark is not as pervasive as that of Matthew and Luke. The reason is obvious: John's story of Jesus does not run parallel to that of Mark as the narratives of Matthew and Luke do. Matthew, Mark, and Luke are called the synoptic gospels because they present the "same' story with only variations in detail and order and the addition of some materials. So they can be placed alongside of one another and "viewed together" (that is what synoptic means) and compared. The first conclusion drawn from this synoptic arrangement was that the first three gospels do not contain independent accounts of Jesus' story, but that the one gospel writer borrowed from the other. The dominant view now is that Mark wrote first and that Matthew and Luke revised Mark's story. Scholars have discovered the theologies of Matthew and Luke by observing how they changed Mark's story.

However, when these scholars returned to the gospel of Mark, they carried back many of the details of the story found only in Matthew and Luke. There are two reasons for this: first, because the synoptic gospels follow the same storyline, it is difficult to keep the details allocated to the appropriate source; second, and perhaps even more important, some of the additions of Matthew and Luke are considered correct interpretations of Mark. In other words many of the additions of Matthew and Luke seemed to make explicit what Mark left implicit, which appeared to grant one permission to read them back into Mark. But what warrant do we have even to read the 'correct' interpretations back into Mark? Should we not first ask why Mark chose to leave these matters implicit, and did not choose to spell them out as Matthew and Luke did?

Of course, some of Matthew and Luke's interpretations went beyond simple clarifications. For example, when Mark called Jesus the Son of God (Mk. 15:39), Matthew and Luke interpreted sonship in a literal and biological sense. It is doubtful that Mark would have accepted their birth stories of Jesus. On the other hand, when Matthew called Jesus Lord in his account of the Stilling of the Storm, Mark would probably have agreed with him although Mark did not call Jesus Lord in his version of the story. Mark merely had the disciples say, "Teacher, do you not care if we perish?" (Mk. 4:38); at the end of the story they asked, "Who then is this, that even the wind and the sea obey him?" (Mk. 4:41). Matthew elevated Jesus from a teacher to Lord and removed the insulting insinuation that he might not care if the disciples perish. That Mark considered Jesus Lord, however, may be deduced from the prophecy about the voice in the wilderness that prepared the way of the Lord (Mk. 1:3).

Matthew clearly indicated that John the Baptist was Elijah. After Jesus told the three disciples that Elijah had come, Matthew added, "Then the disciples understood that he was speaking to them of John the Baptist." (Matt. 17:3). Although there is no doubt that Mark considered John the Baptist Elijah, he nowhere said so outright. Of course, mark considered Jesus the Son of Man at Caesarea Philippi when he had Jesus ask his disciples, "Who do men say that I am?" (Mk 8:27). Matthew included the claim to be the Son of Man in Jesus' question, "Who do men say that the Son of Man is?" (Matt. 16:13). Even where there is essential agreement, to leave a thing unsaid and to say it outright does not amount to the same thing. Besides, there is not always essential agreement.

We have already shown how John had the Spirit descending about the time Mark had it ascending. Luke's view is closer to John's than it is to Mark's. Luke introduced into the synoptic storyline the notion that the Spirit baptism only came after Jesus ascended, so it is not surprising that this view has dominated the interpretation of the gospel of Mark as well. That Mark did not intend to postpone Jesus' spirit baptism until after his departure is indicated by the fact that Mark made Jesus the Spirit baptizer. Instead of " . . . he will baptize you with the Holy Spirit." Acts has " . . . you shall be baptized with the Holy Spirit." (Acts 1:5). Luke did not indicate who the Spirit baptizer would be.

If Jesus were the Spirit baptizer, then Mark understood Jesus' public ministry as a series of Spirit baptisms. Failure to recognize this fact can in part be attributed to the influence of Luke's interpretation on our understanding of Mark. It is also due to the scarcity of references to baptism in Mark. However, no one denies the importance of rebirth in the gospel of John because of the paucity of references to It in that gospel. Rebirth is considered a symbol of a transformation which can be expressed in other terms or images. Why not regard Spirit baptism a symbol which is capable of divergent expressions? In fact Mark called Jesus' passion his baptism (Mk. 10:38). Why not consider the passions of John the Baptist, Jesus, and the early Christians the Spirit baptisms prophesied by John?

The church's story of Jesus was not only shaped by an indiscriminant combination of the four gospel stories, but also by an unwarranted exclusion of a number of apocryphal gospels. The acceptance of the former and the rejection of the latter was not based on their greater or lesser accuracy for both were equally legendary. To include these non-canonical gospels in our synopsis may shed light on obscurities in the story of Jesus that would remain if we continued to study the New Testament gospels in isolation. For example, when we read in the Gospel of Peter about Jesus coming out of the tomb,[161] it suddenly dawns on us that nowhere in the New Testament was Jesus depicted exiting the tomb. It seems that the empty tomb and the appearances were alternate proofs of the resurrection that were only gradually brought into contact with one another.

The order of events—death, burial, resurrection, appearance, and ascension—is probably secondary. The original sequence was probably death, burial, resurrection/ascension, and appearance. In the secondary sequence the ascension followed the appearances, which were located on earth; in the original order the appearances, which were from heaven, followed the ascension. If the spurious ending of Mark (Mk. 16:9-20) were set aside, the only ascension Mark has is that of the Spirit from the cross (Mk. 15:37). Since Mark had Jesus deliver his farewell speech (Mk. 13) before he died, it is doubtful that he intended to relate a resurrection appearance. In the interim between Jesus' death and return, the young man at the tomb simply says, "he is risen, he is not here..." (Mk. 16:6). In his farewell speech Jesus may also have rejected resurrection appearances. Jesus said, "And if anyone says to you, 'Look, here is Christ' or 'Look, there he is' do not believe it." (Mk. 13:21). After rejecting local appearances of Christ, Mark had Jesus point to the coming of the Son of Man in the clouds (Mk. 13:26). In contrast Matthew had the risen Jesus promise the disciples, "... lo, I am with you always, to the close of the age." (Matt. 28:20).

The storyline of the Gospel of Mark has never been fully separated from those of Matthew, Luke, and John. The fusion of the four gospel storylines was based on the assumption that they agreed in fundamentals; although they may have differed on this or that detail, they shared the same guiding Spirit to use the language of the Muratori canon. The immediate effect of excluding the storylines of the other gospels from that of Mark is an apparent loss of meaning, which indicates the extent to which Mark drew its meaning from the other gospels. Although the life of Jesus movement usually based its picture of Jesus on the synoptic gospels (Matthew, Mark, and Luke), when a Christian layman is asked what he believes he almost invariably quotes from the Gospel of John.

With some qualifications Mark may be described as a manifesto inspiring an embattled community in an age of Jewish sectarianism, Matthew a charter organizing a community establishing its separate identity in contrast to formative Judaism, Luke a "popular history" celebrating a stable community that was expanding into the larger world, and John a theology justifying the story of Jesus in terms of the popular Gnostic philosophy of that larger world. There was unity in neither the stories they told nor the communities they addressed. Therefore, we should dispense with gospel harmonizing and read the gospels as four stories instead of one. The gospel truth is that Matthew, mark, Luke, and John, like their apocryphal counter parts, are gospel fictions.

"I myself am an Israelite,
a descendant of Abraham,
a member of the tribe of Benjamin."
(Rom. 11:1)

CHAPTER X

TRUE ISRAEL:
Early "Christianity" As Messianic Judaism

The followers of Jesus did not claim to create a new religion, Christianity, but to represent faithfully the religion into which they were born and to which they continued to belong, "Judaism." The gospel writers and Paul did not intend to replace the sacred scriptures, "the Old Testament," but correctly to interpret them. As with sects in general, the Messianic Jewish sect claimed to represent the traditions more accurately than the dominant Jewish groups of their day. In the Parable of the Vineyard Mark claimed that God rejected the Jewish leaders in favor of the leaders of his own community. Nor was the Markan community the only one to reject the leaders of Israel, and claim to be the bearers of the true Jewish tradition. The Qumran Community rejected the Maccabean rulers because they considered them illegitimate. Qumran claimed to preserve the legitimate Zadok succession abandoned by the Maccabean leaders. So there were a number of different groups or sects claiming to be the true heir of the Jewish traditions: the Pharisees, the Sadducees, the Essenes, and the Zealots. Far from breaking away from their inherited religion, the Jesus movement claimed to be more genuinely Jewish than their fellow countrymen; it was not yet a Christian movement.

Of course, over time the Jesus movement did break away from its Jewish base and developed into an independent religion. Both the Jesus movement and Rabbinic Judaism were forced to abandon the Temple worship after its destruction by the Roman. In contrast the Qumran sect had voluntarily abandoned Temple worship over a century before its destruction. However, all three remained Jewish. The question is, At what point is the Jesus movement no longer Jewish, and why do we call the Jesus movement early Christianity?

As the followers of Jesus developed into a group independent of Judaism, they took the "Old Testament" with them, and came to feel the need to justify their possession of it. Earlier they felt no such need for, as Jewish sectarians, they possessed the scriptures as their rightful inheritance. It was from divergent interpretations of these common scriptures that the various sects arose in the first place. When the Jesus movement abandoned its Jewish base, it had to develop arguments for retaining these old writings, arguments that were not accepted by all (Marcion, for example). My question in regard to the Canon goes in the other direction: If the early Jesus movement was a Jewish sect and wrote much of the New testament, to what extent is the New Testament, itself, a Jewish and not a Christian product?

A famous German work on "primitive Christianity," made the provocative claim that "Jesus was not a 'Christian,' but a Jew."[162] It may now be necessary to add that most of the writings of the New Testament are not Christian, but Jewish. Of course, one can allow that some were Christian if by Christian we mean a Jewish messianic sect and not an independent religion. We are so accustomed to taking for granted that the New Testament is Christian in contrast to the Jewish "Old Testament" that we fail to examine the evidence of the individual writings to see if it supports the claim. Again, of course, the New Testament as a collection was no doubt the product of the Christian Church toward the end of the second century. However, the individual writings of which it is composed already existed prior to their canonization. It is to the history of the New Testament writings and to their content that we have to look to determine the extent to which they are Jewish or Christian.

Of course, we are here dealing with a question of definition that is notoriously difficult and the meaning of both Christianity and Judaism in the first century is up for grabs. J. Andrew Overman, has called the Judaism after the destruction of Jerusalem and the Temple "Formative Judaism."[163] For this same period I would like to suggest that we call the Jesus movement Messianic Judaism, and not Jewish Christianity. If we apply a term such as Christian or Christianity to the writings that came to comprise the New Testament, we should at least consider whether and to what extent they used the term. This should be our guide and not the undoubted fact that these writings were considered Christian by the church toward the end of the second century. If you have by now been driven to consult a concordance, you are probably as shocked as I was to discover how scarce the term Christian is in the "Christian" New Testament.

To understand this oversight one must look at the history of research to discover how scholars were diverted by other concerns. The Christian Church in the nineteenth century, using the tools of historical criticism, searched for the earliest and most genuine tradition on which to base itself. It was so preoccupied with the task of authenticating the events of Jesus life that it failed to notice the anachronism involved in applying the term Christian to this early epoch. To its credit it discovered that Mark was the earliest gospel, distinguished between the genuine letters of Paul and the products of the Pauline school, and identified the Catholic epistles as late. The problem is that by taking as its foundation the earlier works of the New Testament, the Christian Church based itself on works that are more likely to be Jewish, and put on a lower level works that are more likely to be Christian.

While Norman Perrin has the correct perspective in his New Testament Introduction he still read the term Christian into books in which it was not found. In his discussion of Ephesians, a product of the Pauline school, he wrote,

> "It is when we come to Ephesians in the New testament that we must begin to speak of the *Christian* church, with a capital C, and no longer of Christian churches."[164]

Of course Ephesians did not contain the word Christian. Up to this point Perrin had called the Jesus Movement a Jewish Apocalyptic sect some eight or nine times. But prior to this he had already referred to Christian, Christianity, and the Christian church at least 200 times, not always with the proper qualification. Throughout his introduction Perrin used the term Christian several hundred times; *the New Testament, itself, used the word Christian only three times and in only two books* (Acts 11:26, 26:28, and I Pet. 4:16). The first two references may still be to a Jewish sect that included gentiles; only the last reference was probably to Christianity as a movement that was independent of its Jewish base. The writer of Acts claimed that " . . . the disciples were called Christians first in Antioch." (Acts 11:26) A friend of mine who has studied Acts more than I have, noted that Acts did not even claim that the disciples called themselves Christians, but were so called by others.* They were probably called Christians by other Jews because the disciples believed Jesus was the Christ, but that did not make them non-Jewish. In the first century to believe that someone was the messiah suggested that one was Jewish and not something else. At this point Christian or Messianic can still be the designation of a Jewish sect. It was only later and now that belief in Jesus as the Messiah made one Christian and not Jewish.

The second reference to Christian in Acts is found in King Agrippa's reply to Paul's speech to him.

> "Agrippa said to Paul, 'Are you so quickly persuading me to become a Christian?'" (Acts 26:28). R.S.V.

In Hellenistic histories such speeches, if not also their occasions, are known to be fictitious, but there is another problem. Luke implied that Paul was trying to persuade Agrippa to become a Christian, and this runs counter to the non-use of the term Christian not only in the genuine letters of Paul, but also in those of the Pauline school as well. It is a well established principle of Pauline scholarship that when there is a conflict between the account of Paul in Acts and that of Paul's own letters, the latter are to be preferred.[165]

Perrin's "Christian" interpretation of the New Testament led him to misread a central concept in Paul's theology. One of Perrin's section headings reads,

> "PAUL AS A MISSIONARY, FIRST JEWISH, THEN CHRISTIAN."

Again, it must be emphasized that Paul never used the term Christian; instead he wrote, "To the Jew first and also to the *Greek*." (Rom. 1:16; 2:9, 10).[166]

The third and final use of the term Christian in the New Testament is in I Peter in which he writes about those who suffer "as a Christian." (I Peter 4:16). Here we probably have to do with Christianity as a movement independent of Judaism. The introduction to I Peter in the R.S.V claims that the "Christianity" reflected in the letter "is not struggling to define itself in relationship to Jewish traditions. The letter assumes that the church is the true heir of the covenant (2:4-10)." The ones who suffer as Christians were probably Gentiles since the author claimed they " . . . . have already spent enough time doing what the Gentiles like to do . . ." (I Pet. 4:3), and, said their persecutors " . . . are surprised that you no longer join them in the same excesses of dissipation . . ." (I Pet. 4:4). When gentiles came to predominate in the

Christian movement, it became a separate religion from Judaism.

The Jew / gentile antithesis (ethnic) played a more fundamental role in defining Christianity as a separate religion than the other dichotomies such as Jewish and Hellenistic (cultural and political), Hebrew and Greek (linguistic), and synagogue and church (religious institutional). One did not have to abandon "Judaism" to be hellenized, speak Greek, or belong to the church. The biggest distinction between the Old and New Testaments is linguistic not ethnic. While the former was written almost exclusively in Hebrew (the book of Daniel has Aramaic sections), the latter was written exclusively in Greek. This change in language did not signify a shift in the ethnicity of the authors. The Jews produced an extensive literature in the Greek language including a Greek translation of the "Old Testament," the Septuagint (LXX). While the Tanak, Hebrew Bible, led directly to the Mishna and Formative Judaism, the Septuagint, Greek Bible, led to the "New Testament" and Messianic Judaism.

Secondly, the adoption of Hellenistic cultural and political institutions did not make one non-Jewish. The Hellenistic states not only encouraged the adoption of the Greek language, but also instituted an extensive program of Hellenization through the building of Greek cities in Palestine.[167] By "New Testament" times all Jewish sects were more or less Hellenized, but that did not make them non-Jewish. Many Jews wrote histories in a Hellenistic style: Josephus and Luke/Acts.

Thirdly, the adoption of Greek terms for one's group did not make one non-Jewish. Both synagogue and church originated in the Hellenistic period and used a Greek term for a gathering (synagogue), and an assembly (church/ecclesia). Therefore, Matthew's use of the word church does not imply a non-Jewish Christian group. Church was simply the Greek term for a Jewish assembly that believed that Jesus was the Messiah, as synagogue was the alternate Greek term for a Jewish gathering that did not believe Jesus was the Messiah. At first synagogue and ecclesia / church were Greek terms for the gathering or assembly of two different sects within "Judaism." Actually, they reflect the factionalism that preceded the formation of Judaism as well as Christianity.

If neither the adoption of the Greek language and culture, nor the belief in Christ, nor the use of the term Christian or church made one non-Jewish, what did? What gave Jesus' followers the consciousness of being Christian as opposed to being Jewish? In my opinion this separation came about as a result of the influx of gentiles into the Jesus movement. Those who suffered as Christians in I Peter were gentiles. With this shift in the ethnic composition of the Jesus messianic sect came the consciousness of their separation from Judaism. Of course, this process was hastened by the destruction of Jerusalem and the Temple. Before the war with Rome, the Synagogue and Church were held together by the Temple worship.

Norman Perrin has correctly pointed out that not enough attention has been paid to the influence of the fall of Jerusalem on the development of both Judaism and Christianity.[168] Prior to the war with Rome there were a number of different sects: Pharisees, Sadducees, Essenes, Zealots, Jesus' followers and others. With the fall of the Temple, the power base of the Sadducean priesthood was destroyed, causing them to disappear from the scene. The Qumran (Essene) community suffered a similar fate when their monastery was destroyed by the Romans. The Pharisees survived as Rabbinic Judaism and the Jesus movement as Messianic Judaism. Because neither was dependent on the Temple, they made the transition to the synagogue and church. The number of sects was drastically reduced by the war. In order to understand the gospels we must relate them to these events that were happening when they were written.

Too often we view the gospels together (synoptically); instead we should view them successively (historically). This synoptic comparison of the gospels has led to a distortion in our view of them. For example, Matthew is often described as the most Jewish of the gospels as compared with Mark, Luke and John. In my opinion this is an illusion because Matthew was closer to the Judaism that developed after the destruction of the Temple and the Judaism we know today. Mark may very well more genuinely reflect the Judaism that existed prior to the destruction of Jerusalem and the Temple. The differences between Mark and Matthew are usually thought to represent different communities in different localities rather than the same community at different times. It is likely that Matthew, who early came into possession of a copy of Mark, belonged to the same Jewish sect or group as he. If they did not belong to the same group, it would be necessary to explain how Matthew came to use Mark as a source. The differences between them can be explained at least in part by the circumstance that Mark reflected the pre-war and war time situation, and Matthew the post war context. In Mark Jesus' enemies were the scribes, and chief Priests. In Matthew Jesus' enemies become the Pharisees.[169] The Chief Priests are gone. Matthew reflects the Judaism that was developing at Jamnia, which was led by the Pharisees. Mark mentioned the synagogue and the Temple, but not the church. Matthew mentioned the church. Whereas in Mark Jesus was on friendly terms with some Pharisees, in Matthew they are implacable enemies. This opposition reflected the tension between Matthew's community and the developing Judaism of the post war period.

Since Mark lived under the laws of the Temple state, he did not feel the need to set up a rule for his community. In Mark Jesus had a leper he cleansed to show himself to the priests as Moses commanded and Jesus proceeded to interpret the common (Torah) law. When the Temple state disappeared, Matthew did feel the need to set up a rudimentary rule for his community and a process for disciplining its members (Matt. 18:15-20). Qumran had set up a Community Rule earlier because they withdrew from the Temple state and became a self-governing monastic community. These new community rules, Matthew's and Rabbinic Judaism's, were imposed on their community only and not on the nation as a whole. Mark still envisioned a theocracy under the rule of God and the Messiah, which included all of Israel and the gentiles as well. In Matthew the Kingdom of God became the Kingdom of Heaven and on earth the church, which was to be ruled by the ones to whom the keys were given.

This question of the place of the Jesus movement and Mark's group in the Temple State suggests a role for Jesus that has received far too little attention. With the reputation of lawyers at an all time low it may not be the best time to suggest that Jesus was, among other things, a Jewish lawyer. Of course, he was also a healer (doctor) and teacher. It was not an age of specialization. But it cannot be denied that an enormous amount of his time was spent interpreting the Jewish law. The variety of legal questions that came before him was astonishing. Prior to the destruction of the Temple the law that Jesus was interpreting was the law of the land; after the fall of Jerusalem the law became the rule for the community both in Rabbinic Judaism and Messianic Judaism. In Mark Jesus referred to "what Moses commanded." (Mk. 1:44); in Matthew Jesus referred to what he, himself, commanded: "Teaching them to observe all things whatsoever I have commanded you . . ." (Matt. 28:20).

APPENDIX

THE MESSIAH:
God's Son Not David's

Since the Messiah is now generally regarded as the Son of David by both Jews and Christians, it is surprising that Mark does not share this common opinion. It was frequently asserted that Mark retained the notion of the Davidic descent of the Messiah and the title Son of David for Jesus purged of its nationalistic associations, and elevated to a higher level. It will be the contention of this appendix that Mark rejected the title Son of David altogether and had Jesus claim that the Messiah was God's son not David's.

> "While Jesus was teaching in the temple, he said, "How can the scribes say that the Messiah is the son of David? David himself, by the Holy Spirit declared,
> > 'the Lord said to my Lord, "Sit at my right hand, until I put your enemies under your feet."'
>
> David himself calls him Lord; so how can he be his son?" and the large crowd was listening to him with delight." (RSV Mk. 12:35-37).

The traditional belief that Jesus was a descendent of David, has led to a distorted and contradictory pattern of commentary on this passage: The commentator first acknowledges the straight forward meaning of these verses, refers to the traditional view, and then rejects the obvious explanation in favor of the traditional one.

Anticipating his rejection of the obvious meaning of the passage, Branscomb asserted, "This is a strange and difficult passage."[170] Following the above pattern he first acknowledged its plain meaning.

> "Jesus attacks the teaching of the scribes that the Christ is David's son, and affirms instead that he is David's Lord."[171]

Then he referred to the traditional belief as to Jesus' descent.

> But what is denied is exactly what Christians from Paul's day on believed—namely that Jesus was a descendant of David (see Rom. I:3, and the genealogies in Matt. and Luke).[172]

Finally, he rejected the obvious meaning of the passage.

> "By the time he (Mark) wrote, belief in the Davidic lineage of Jesus was no doubt current throughout the Christian movement. Mark certainly did not doubt it."[173]

A more recent commentator, Hugh Anderson, followed the same pattern. First he acknowledged the plain sense of the passage.

> "If the saying, of verse 35^b-37 is authentic, it is most natural to suppose that in debate with his opponents Jesus was defending the (non-Davidic) character of his Messiahship against the popular Jewish recognition that Messiah must be of David's line."[174]

Then he also referred to the traditional view.

> "... the early church ... universally accepted the Davidic descent of Jesus ... and had apparently no objection to 'Son of David' as a title for Jesus (Mt. 1:6, Lk. 2:4; 3:31; Rom. 1:3; 2Tim. 2:8).[175]

Anderson then rejected the plain meaning of the passage asserting that, "... the Hellenistic church saw in it the evidence that Jesus was not just Son of David but Son of God (cf. 15:39)."[176]

Anderson raised two issues, which should be distinguished: the Davidic descent of the Messiah and "Son of David" as a title for the Messiah. Two other issues also need to be distinguished: the Davidic descent of the *Messiah* and the Davidic descent of Jesus. The designation, "Son of David" appears to have originated with Mark—in the New Testament at least—and was passed on to Matthew and Luke. It also appears to be limited to the synoptic gospels (Mk. 10:47, 10:48, and 12:35; Mt. 1:1, 1:20, 12:23, 15:22, 20:30, 20:31, 21:9, 21:15, 22:42; Lk. 3:31, 18:38, and 18:39).

The strongest affirmation of the Davidic descent of the Messiah is found in Schweizer's commentary on Mark. After conceding that "... the easiest interpretation of the statement." is, "... that he (Jesus) is disputing the Davidic descent of the Messiah."[177] Schweizer goes on to claim,

> "The Davidic descent of the Messiah, however, is not denied in the Christian writings prior to the Epistle of Barnabas (12:10f.), and there it occurred as the result of an anti-Jewish attitude. Otherwise Jesus is regarded universally as David's descendant."[178]

What Schweizer failed to say was how seldom the Davidic descent of the Messiah was affirmed. A glance at a concordance will reveal how infrequently David is even mentioned in the New Testament at least—in only nine of the 27 books. Therefore, it does not appear to be true that

Jesus was universally acknowledged as David's descendant. If Mark denied the Davidic descent of Jesus, then Schweizer's other claim that Barnabas was the first to deny it would also be inaccurate.

Finally, we come to an author who at first seems to appreciate the full force of Mark's argument. Tolbert's is by far the best and most complete analysis of Mark's / Jesus' reasoning. She claims rightly that this saying is cast in the form of an enthymeme or rhetorical syllogism (a truncated form of argument ordinarily used in public speaking) in which the major premise was omitted. Because the premise was a belief shared by the audience and speaker, it was simply left unstated.

Syllogisms and enthymemes differ in at least two respects. First the syllogism is more complete exhibiting the major premise, minor premise and conclusion. Second, it utilizes as premises notions that are universally agreed upon.

> Major premise: All men are mortal
> Minor premise: Socrates is a man.
> Conclusion: Socrates is mortal.

Enthymemes substitute for these universal propositions common opinions, folk wisdom, or probable truths that are more likely to be culturally and historically conditioned. Therefore, the conclusions drawn are only probable.

For example, an enthymeme/syllogism can be formed from the proverbial saying, "Spare the rod and spoil the child." (Prov. 13:24).

> Major premise: Parents who do not use the rod to
>   discipline their children spoil them.
> Minor premise: Mrs. Jones did not use the rod on
>   her children.
> Conclusion: Mrs. Jones spoiled her children.

The rod was a rather harsh instrument of discipline, the use of which we would probably consider child abuse now. Paul said he was beaten with rods three times (2 Cor. 11:25). The enthymeme/syllogism we would form from such information would be quite different.

> Major premise: Parents who use the rod to discipline their children abuse them by teaching them to solve problems by resorting to violence.
> Minor premise: Mrs. Jones used the rod to correct her children.
> Conclusion: Mrs. Jones abused her children.

Unlike Jesus' / Mark's audience, the gospel's modern readers may not find the premises, whether expressed or unexpressed, so obvious, the Davidic authorship of Psalm 110, for example. Therefore, Tolbert was right to reconstruct the full syllogism or complete logical form of the argument underlying the enthymeme. According to Tolbert,

> "... Jesus interprets an accepted messianic text enthymematically. He begins by stating the view of the scribes, which he intends to refute, 'that the Christ is the son of David' (12:35) and then constructs his scriptural enthymeme with a suppressed major premise drawn from customary mores:
>
> Suppressed major premise: Fathers do not address their sons with titles of respect like "sir" or "master."
> Minor premise: David declared "The Lord said to my master, 'Sit at my right hand, till I put your enemies under your feet.'" (Mk. 12:36).
>
> Conclusion: The one David calls master cannot be his son.

Because fathers do not call their sons master, David's

reference to the Christ as my master (or "my lord") proves that the Christ cannot be David's son *in any traditional sense.* It is possible to understand Jesus as "Son of David" only if one recognizes that title as describing one aspect of Jesus' broader role as heir of the vineyard." To this conclusion that the messiah cannot be David's son Tolbert adds a number of qualifications. The messiah cannot be David's son "in any traditional sense," unless it is combined with "Jesus' broader role as heir of the vineyard," and with no "literal attempt to trace Davidic lineage as a test of messiahship."[179] None of these qualifications are found in Mark. She is right when she writes, "The Christ is God's heir, not David's."[180]. However, this accurate statement has to be contrasted with an opposite affirmation made by her elsewhere.

> "Chapter 10: Jesus the Heir of the Vineyard will discuss the parable of the Tenants and the dominant portrayal of Jesus in Division Two as the true heir, the Son of David, the authoritative interpreter of Jewish Scripture and tradition."[181]

Like other commentators Tolbert, after acknowledging the plain meaning of the passage, proceeded to reject it.

Tolbert performed identical operations on two previous enthymemes in Mark: the one about paying taxes to Caesar (Mk. 12:13-17),[182] and the one about the resurrection (Mk. 12:18-27).[183] In these two instances she simply accepted Mark's conclusions without qualification, apparently because she found nothing controversial in them.

The most consistent interpretation of this passage is that of Werner Kelber. He claimed that Mark rejected the Davidic descent of the messiah, and pointed out that Mark also rejected Bartimaeus' hailing of Jesus as the Son of David by representing him as blind when he uttered the confession. Finally, when Jesus entered Jerusalem, the crowd shouted, "Blessed is the coming Kingdom of our father David." (Mk.

11:10). Kelber contrasted the kingdom of their father David with the kingdom of Jesus' father God.[184]

However, it is Tolbert's concept of Jesus as the heir of the vineyard that explains why Mark rejected the Davidic descent of the messiah. To say that Jesus as God's son inherited the vineyard was to say that the Jewish leaders as David's sons did not. They were simply tenants of the vineyard. When the tenants killed the beloved son, the vineyard passed not to them, but to Jesus' family the ones who did the will of God—the Markan community!

These authors, except for Kelber, rejected Mark's conclusion in regard to the Messiah's lineage because they viewed the gospel through the set of beliefs shaped by Formative Rabbinical Judaism and Matthaean Sectarian Judaism. There is no doubt about the prevalence of the belief in the Davidic descent of the Messiah among the scribes (of the Pharisees) and Paul, who was also a Pharisee. Apparently Matthew agreed with Formative Judaism against Mark on this point. In fact Matthew's most drastic revision of Mark was to add a genealogy to Mark's narrative showing Jesus' descent from David.

However, Mark represented the period preceding the war between Rome and Judea in which a number of alternative messianic notions still existed. The Essenes at Qumran, for example, expected a messiah or messiahs of Aaron and Israel.[185] To understand how these various messianic notions arose one must go back to the history and stream(s) of tradition, what Greg Riley called the River of God. The Davidic dynasty came to an end in the Exile which for some groups weakened the connection between the house of David and the Messianic hope.

With the return from the Exile, the rebuilding of the temple, and the concentration on the Torah, priest and scribes came to fill the power vacuum. The returning community was led by Ezra, a scribe not a royal prince. It was a family of priests who sparked the Maccabean revolt, and the subsequent power struggles revolved around priest not kings. That explains how the Essenes came to expect a messiah of Aaron and the book of Hebrews called Jesus a High Priest (Heb. 4:14-5:14) as well as the Son of God. Though Hebrews mentioned the tribe of Judah, it has nothing about the Davidic descent of Jesus. Like Mark, Hebrews preferred the title Son of God and did not mention the title Son of David. The author went so far as to specifically reject genealogies (Matthew / Luke) in favor of Jesus' priesthood being like that of Melchisedek, who had neither father nor mother (Heb. 7;3). Like Mark, Hebrews emphasized that Jesus as the son of God was heir as opposed to Moses, who was a servant (Heb. 3:5-6).

In addition to this indigenous priestly role for the messiah there were other models suggested by the surrounding cultures. Mark called the Messiah the Son of Man and the Son of God, which probably reflected Persian and Hellenistic conceptions. Zoroastrian eschatology tended to emphasize divine Saviors, like the Son of Man in Daniel and Mark, instead of earthly deliverers like David. Similarly, Hellenistic religion tended to elevate great earthly leaders, like Alexander the Great and some Roman Caesars to divine status. Since Mark's eschatology, like Persian eschatology, led him to emphasize the messiah's divine connections, it is not surprising that he rejected the notion that the messiah was the Son of David.

APPENDIX 2

THE GUIDING PRINCIPLE OF MARK'S GOSPEL:
Elijah Must Come First

Introduction

According to Albert Schweitzer in the time of Jesus the Jews were expecting the appearance, not of the Messiah, but Elijah, the forerunner.[1] Superficially read, the evidence appears to support Schweitzer's view. When Jesus' name became known through the preaching of the Twelve, the people believed that he was John the Baptist, Elijah, or one of the prophets. The conscience ridden King Herod thought Jesus was John the Baptist whom he had beheaded (Mk. 6:14-16). When Jesus at Caesarea Philippi asked the disciples, "Who do people say that I am?" They answered, "John the Baptist; and others, Elijah; and still others, one of the prophets." (Mk. 8:27-30). Since no proportions are given one cannot conclude from these passages how widespread each belief was.

Some scholars have recently called into question the notion that the belief that Elijah would be the forerunner of the Messiah was widely held by the Jews in the time of Jesus. They point out how little evidence there is for it outside the gospels.[2] Since the notion in Mark arises from messianic speculation, it may not be found among non-messianic Jews. The belief in the first coming of Elijah is based on a messianic reading of a passage in the last book of the Old Testament,"Lo, I will send you the prophet Elijah before the great and terrible day of the LORD comes." (Mal. 4:4)

Non-messianic Jewish exegesis took this passage to

mean that Elijah would return before the Day of the LORD God; messianic interpretation concluded that Elijah would return before the Day of the LORD Jesus. Mark may have been right when he attributed to the scribes the belief in the return of Elijah before the End time, but it was probably Mark and his community who made Elijah the messenger and forerunner of the Messiah (Mk. 9:11).

For Mark the first coming of Elijah was the guiding principle of the gospel which necessarily preceded the question of Christology, for if Elijah had not come, Jesus was simply not the Messiah. Any doubting or denying that Elijah had come constituted a questioning or rejecting of Jesus' messiahship. Just as Elijah must come first, Mark must first establish that Elijah has already come. That is why Mark's gospel began with the messenger prophecy (Mk. 1:2-3). The principle of the first coming of Elijah was so important to Mark that he repeated it twice in the messenger prophecy, placed Elijah before Moses at the Transfiguration (Mk. 9:4), explained it to the three disciples as they descended the mountain (Mk. 9:9-13), and even mentioned Elijah in the crucifixion scene in which bystanders heard Jesus say, "Elijah, Elijah, why have you forsaken me?" (Mk. 15:34).

When Mark attributed the belief in the first coming of Elijah to the scribes, he began to reveal the conclusions he had drawn from this "guiding principle (Αρχη) of the gospel. In other references to Elijah Mark demonstrated that the people consistently rejected Jesus' equation of John the Baptist with Elijah, and also rejected Jesus' messianic claims.

In order to show how this "debate" determined the form of Mark's argument and generated the structure of the gospel, it will be necessary to offer a revision of the first three verses of Mark, and suggest that they constitute the introduction to his persuasive discourse. This introduction will then be compared to the prooemium of that other persuasive discourse or word of exhortation, the book of Hebrews (Heb. 1:1-4).

Mark's / Jesus' "Debate" With The Scribes: Has Elijah Already Come?

> "As they were coming down the mountain, he ordered them to tell no one about what they had seen, until after the Son of Man had risen from the dead. So they kept the matter to themselves, questioning what this rising from the dead could mean. Then they asked him, 'Why do the scribes say that Elijah must come first?' He said to them, 'Elijah is indeed coming first to restore all things. How then is it written about the Son of Man, that he is to go through many sufferings and be treated with contempt? But I tell you that Elijah has come, and they did to him whatever they pleased, as it is written about him.'" (Mk. 9:9-13).

The opinion that Mark had Jesus attribute to the scribes constituted a denial that Jesus was the Messiah because Elijah had not yet come. Since Mark / Jesus agreed with the scribes that Elijah must come first, the "debate" was about whether Elijah had already come. Mark / Jesus argued that John the Baptist was Elijah, but throughout the gospel the scribes and others refused to accept this identification. Even Jesus' own disciples quoted the scribes' objection to what Jesus had just said, and Mark, unlike Matthew, did not say that they understood after Jesus' explanation.

One gets the impression that Matthew objected to Mark's account on the basis of both form and content. Leaving aside Matthew's stylistic changes, we will concentrate only on those of substance. In Mark's account of the Transfiguration Elijah was mentioned before Moses (Mk. 9:4); In Matthew's account Moses was placed first before Elijah restoring their chronological order (Matt. 17:3). When Jesus replied to the disciples' question about the scribal tradition, he said, "Elijah has come," and Matthew added, "and they did not recognize him" (Matt. 17:12). Matthew understood that Jesus was speaking about John the Baptist, but he noticed that Mark had not said that the disciples understood.

This left the impression that the disciples remained on the side of the scribes, who did not consider John Elijah. Therefore, Matthew added, "Then the disciples understood that he was speaking to them about John the Baptist." (Matt. 17:13). Matthew clearly spelled out that "they," the scribes, did not consider John the Baptist Elijah, but that the disciples did.

In the second century the subject of the first coming of Elijah resurfaced in St. Justin Martyr's *Dialogue with Trypho, the Jew*.

> "And Trypho said, 'You seem to me to be ready to answer any of my questions, thanks to your extensive exchange in debates with many persons on every possible topic.[3]

One of the topics was the first coming of Elijah.

> Trypho says, "…from the fact that Elijah has not yet come, I must declare that this man (Jesus) is not the Christ."[4]

Justin Martyr answered,

> Wherefore did our Christ, who was on earth at this time, reply to those who were saying that Elijah must come before the appearance of Christ, 'Elijah indeed is to come and will restore all things. But I say to you that Elijah has come already, and they did not know him, but did to him whatever they wished. And it is added, Then the disciples understood that he had spoken to them of John the Baptist.[5]

The scribes were not the only ones who failed to recognize that John the Baptist was Elijah. Elijah is mentioned in contexts that imply that the people also reject this identification. When Herod heard about Jesus, he thought that he was John the Baptist risen from the dead. The people thought he was John the Baptist, Elijah, or one of the prophets. In any case this would tend to negate the identification of John the Baptist with Elijah (Mk. 6:14-15). Similarly, when Jesus asked the disciples on the way to Caesarea Philippi, "Who do people say that I am?", their reply was virtually identical to the opinions of the people when Herod heard about Jesus (Mk. 8:27-28). Therefore, the same conclusion can be drawn, namely, that the people did not consider John the Baptist Elijah.

Again in the Temple when the Jewish leaders were questioning Jesus' authority, and Jesus challenged them to declare themselves in regard to John's baptism, they refused. They would not say John's baptism was of human origin for fear of the people. Then Mark added, "for all regarded John as truly a prophet" (Mk. 11:32), but not Elijah!

Finally, Mark introduced the Elijah issue into the crucifixion scene. In Mark Jesus cried from the cross, "My God, My God, why have you forsaken me?" (Mk. 15:34). Apologetic interests have so dominated the interpretation of this verse that some have suggested that Jesus quoted the entire Psalm 22 from which this saying was taken, which ended on a positive note. However, if we read the saying in the context of the gospel of Mark, we realize that Mark focused on a seemingly irrelevant misunderstanding on the part of the people gathered around the cross. Because of the similarity of sounds in the original languages in the place of "My God, My God, why have you forsaken me?", the people heard, "Elijah, Elijah, why have you forsaken me?" If Mark created this scene, as I believe he did, this misunderstanding and not Psalm 22 may contain the point he was making. Once again, if the people thought that Elijah might "come to take him down" from the cross, they did not consider John Elijah (Mk. 15:34-36).

In the dialogue that followed the Transfiguration Jesus referred to the scriptures twice—"how then is it written," and "as it is written about him" (Mk. 9:12-13)—but no quotations followed. Elsewhere I argued that both references were to the messenger prophecy at the beginning of Mark.[6] A more convincing argument for a link between the prophecy and the dialogue is their common subject. If the subject of the conversation between Jesus and his disciples on descending the mountain of Transfiguration was the first coming of Elijah, then the references in it to unspecified scriptures were to the messenger prophecy, because the first coming of Elijah was also the subject of that prophecy.

Scholars have usually understood the messenger prophecy (Mk. 1:2-3) in terms of a prophecy and its fulfillment, but in the context of the debate with the scribes it assumed the form of an argument for Jesus' messiahship. Therefore, for Mark the first coming of Elijah became "The guiding principle (αρχη) of the gospel of Jesus Christ, Son of God."(Mk. 1:1). The importance this principle had for Mark is unmistakable in that he repeated it four times: in the messenger prophecy he has the messenger / you, and the voice / Lord; in the following narrative John / Jesus and in the above dialogue Elijah / Son of Man.

Mark Answers the Scribes: John Was Elijah

When Mark had Jesus explain to his disciples that Elijah had come first, he presented a conclusion to a tightly reasoned argument that began with the first word of Mark, αρχη, which is usually translated beginning. Translators believed that Mark intended αρχη to refer to the beginning of the gospel story; In contrast we will translate αρχη as "(The) guiding principle" and take it to indicate the starting-point of a reasoned discourse. In another move translators put a period after the first line of Mark and consider it the title of the gospel. We will move this period to just after the "Isaiah (sic)" quotation and take the first three verses of Mark to be the introduction to his persuasive discourse. Finally, we will add the verb "to be" just after the introduction to the quotation, which will make the messenger prophecy "(The) guiding principle of the gospel of Jesus Christ Son of God."

αρχη as the Chronological Beginning of the Gospel Story

If we are to make a case for taking the first word of Mark (αρχη) as the logical starting-point of the gospel of Mark, we must first explain why it has for so long been considered the chronological beginning of that gospel. As Mark was translated into the English language, the first word of the gospel (αρχη) was rendered as "(the) beginning" of the gospel story. Because Mark's first interpreters, Matthew and Luke, converted Mark's topical order into a chronological sequence, Mark's gospel has from the first century been read as a story, the gospel story. Since a story required a chronological starting-point, αρχη was understood as its temporal beginning. In the eighteenth and nineteenth centuries historians came to view Mark as a historical or biographical account, which also required a chronological beginning. With the shift from a historical to a literary study of Mark, there was no change in the meaning assigned to αρχη because even a fictional story required a chronological beginning.

However, problems arose when scholars attempted to specify the exact point of this beginning. According to Elaine Pagels, "Mark opens his gospel by telling of Jesus' baptism..."[7] This oversight is pardonable because her very excellent book is not primarily about the gospel of Mark. Mark's gospel does not begin with the appearance of John the Baptist; it begins with an announcement of the gospel and an appeal to prophecy. The Scholars Bible translation of Mark acknowledged the messenger prophecy as the beginning of the gospel, "The good news of Jesus the anointed begins with something Isaiah the prophet wrote:"[8]

> In order to accomplish this feat the translator was obliged to change a Greek noun, "beginning (αρχη)" into a verb "begins".

Another commentator who interpreted the first word of Mark, αρχη, chronologically, felt compelled to link verse one to verse four in which John's story began. He considered the intervening prophecy of verses two and three parenthetical. This is clearly revealed in his proposed translation of Mark 1: 1-4.

"The starting-point of the Good News about Jesus Christ (in accordance with the scriptural words of the Prophet Isaiah, "The voice of a man crying in the desert, 'Make ye ready the way of the Lord, Make straight his paths.'"), was John, who baptized in the desert, and proclaimed a baptism of repentance with a view to remission of sins."

By placing the verb "to be" after the prophecy and a period after verse four, Rawlinson created a long sentence in which the prophecy is treated as a parenthesis. In an apparent effort to reduce the size of the parenthetical element to make it more acceptable this translation omitted Mark 1: 2b,

> Behold, I send my messenger before thy face, who shall prepare thy way;[9]

Another consequence of interpreting αρχη as the beginning of a story is the tendency to extend the introduction so as to incorporate as many of the story elements as possible. The arrangement of the Greek text of Mark by Westcott and Hort suggested that Mark's introduction extended only through verse eight. R.H. Lightfoot and James M. Robinson expanded Mark's introduction through verse thirteen.[10] Others suggested that Mark's introduction ended at verse fifteen.[11] This enlarged introduction accurately reflected the underlying story in Mark, but did not adequately account for the persuasive discourse that framed the gospel.

When I wrote my book, *Mark A Twice-Told Tale*, I treated Mark as a story. That is why I utilized the parable of the Vineyard to cast light on the gospel's story elements, since the parable recapitulated so much of the gospel story. However, such a choice also ignored the persuasive discourse that dominated the gospel.[12] A better choice would have been the messenger prophecy. In fact I did show how elements of the prophecy, such as the desert, the way etc., extended throughout the gospel in such a way as to virtually generate its structure. However, my conception of the messenger prophecy as a passion prophecy prevented me from then realizing the full significance of its role in ordering the Markan discourse.

It will be seen that my choice of the messenger prophecy as the text of Mark's persuasive discourse is in line with the practice of Robinson and other scholars of choosing a short passage in Mark by which to reveal the meaning of the gospel. In my book I attributed this procedure to the undue influence of the pulpit on the study.[13] However, since the study of rhetoric saturated Mark's environment, his use of a text in the preacher's sense of a short passage in order to launch his "sermon" may have been due to the influence of the ancient *pulpit or lectern.*

Another question deserves at least a brief mention: Why have Bible translators not resorted to the logical meaning of αρχη? In the first place many "translations" are revisions of the King James Version, which is, itself, a revision of earlier translations. Recent revisers' two main concerns were to correct the manuscript base and to update the language where words had changed their meaning. An example of the second concern is the word gospel, whose meaning is no longer common knowledge, being replaced by the translation "good news." Also Holy Ghost is now translated as Holy Spirit. In the case of "beginning" the meaning of the word remained the same from King James' day until now; it was just not the best translation in the first place. Even in the case of a modern "translation" such as Goodspeed's New Testament, which rearranged the books in chronological order beginning with I Thessalonians, and is touted to be a new translation, the influence of the King James Version and its revisers is discernable.

αρχη as the Guiding Principle of a Persuasive Discourse

The *guiding principle* of the good news of Jesus Christ, the Son of God, as it is written in the prophet Isaiah, *is as follows*:

> "See, I am sending my messenger ahead of you,
> who will prepare your way;
> the voice of one crying out in the wilderness:
> 'Prepare the way of the Lord,
> make his paths straight.'"
> (Mk. 1: 1-3, RSV).

Using The New Oxford Annotated Bible, I have made only necessary changes: αρχη is translated as "The guiding principle" instead of "The beginning", after "the Son of God" I placed a comma instead of a period, and after "make his paths straight I placed a period instead of a comma. Finally, I added the words "is as follows" after "the prophet Isaiah," creating a complete sentence in which "The guiding principle" is the subject and the messenger prophecy is the predicate.

Interpretation through Punctuation

Since the Greek manuscripts of Mark contain no punctuation, the addition of periods and commas etc. is an act of interpretation. In regard to the passage in question there is considerable disagreement as to how it is to be punctuated. The most important choice has to do with the placement of the period because it indicates the extent of the sentence. I have chosen to place the period after verse three and consider the first three verses the introduction of Mark, not the introduction of the gospel story, but the prooemium of a persuasive discourse.

Those who place the period after verse one usually consider it the title of the gospel. Some have even gone so far as to suggest that αρχη, beginning, was added later converting the Greek word for gospel from a nominative to a genitive. Originally it would have simply read "The Gospel of Jesus Christ" instead of "The Beginning of the Gospel of Jesus Christ."[14] My solution does not require such a speculative reconstruction of the text.

Finally, before the messenger prophecy I have chosen to place the words "as follows" instead of a colon[15] to make the meaning more explicit. The variety of punctuation used elsewhere in the passage affect its meaning less than the above instances. Of course, I reject the notion that the messenger prophecy is parenthetical.

To Be or Not to Be: The Omission of the Verb "To Be" in the Greek Sentence.

Nigel Turner points out that it was a fairly common practice in constructing the Greek sentence to omit the verb "to be", which was viewed as a weak copula that could easily be supplied. After conceding that it made good sense to add the verb "to be" to the first three verses of Mark, he decided against it on purely statistical grounds.[16] In my opinion by translating αρχη as "guiding principle" instead of "beginning", the addition of the verb "to be" to the passage once again becomes a viable option.

αρχη as a Guiding Principle

By far the most important change I have made in this passage is to translate the Greek word αρχη as "guiding principle". Although it remains a minority opinion, there is some support for it. While a few authors have recognized that "governing principle" or "rule" etc. is a possible translation of αρχη, no one, to my knowledge has systematically drawn the implications of doing so. They continue to operate with the translation "beginning" which has strong chronological connotations and even confuse it with the term rule which carries the alternate logical meaning. Witness this fusion or confusion of the two meanings in the following quotation from a recent commentary.

> *The beginning*: In Greek *arche* can mean "starting point, foundation, origin," and even "rule," or "governing principle." The meaning in Mark 1:1 is linked to whether a period or a comma is placed after "Son of God." In the former case v. 1 is a kind of title or *incipit* to the whole work, whereas in the latter case the beginning is in the fulfillment of the prophecy quoted in vv.2-3 ("The beginning . . . as it is written . . ."). Our translation interprets v. 1 as a title for the whole work, so that the faith and proclamation of Mark's community have both their "beginning" and "rule" of interpretation in the story of Jesus about to unfold.[17]

From this quotation it is clear that punctuation and interpretation go hand in hand. It is also clear that their preference for the chronological term "beginning" is conditioned by their understanding of Mark as ". . . the story of Jesus about to unfold." Even so they are reluctant to give up completely the benefits conferred by the term bearing the logical meaning, so they opt for a coordination of the two terms "beginning" and "rule".

Ernest Best in his book *Mark The Gospel As Story* also attempts to have it both ways.

> That the book however is a verbal statement of the gospel is true whether we understand 'the beginning' in v. 1. to refer either to John the Baptizer (vv. 2-8), to the Prologue (vv. 2-13 or vv. 2-15), to the earthly life of Jesus as the beginning of the Christian movement, or give the word the meaning 'origin' or 'principle'.[18]

He lays all of these choices along side one another as if the "verbal statement of the gospel" would remain the same regardless of which alternative one chose. We will soon see what a difference it makes.

A final attempt to combine the two terms is found in a "popular" work on Mark.

> Indeed, Mark alone begins with a reference to the 'beginning' or 'first principle', and then an expounding of 'the way of the Lord' in line with the Solomonic wisdom in Proverbs addressed to the son."[19]

Did he forget John 1:1? "In the beginning (αρχη) was the word . . ." While Horne linked the 'beginning' or 'first principle' with one element of the prophecy that followed, "the way of the Lord," he did not relate it to the other themes of the prophecy which appear throughout Mark: the desert, the messenger, and the Lord. When we include all of these elements, we see the connection not only between "the guiding principle" and the prophecy but also between the prophecy and the rest of the gospel. Just as the messenger prepared the way of the Lord in the prophecy, John prepared the way of Jesus in the gospel.

Finally, Willi Marxsen paved the way for the logical translation of αρχη as guiding principle rather than chronological beginning by observing that the connection between events in Mark was not temporal but topical. Writing about the different blocks of material on "Jesus—the Baptist—the Old Testament", Marxsen claimed,

> The connection is topical, that is, it is made from a theological or, strictly speaking, Christological point of view."[2]

If I understand his comment on the term αρχη, Marxsen preferred the logical to the chronological meaning of the word. Concerning this term he wrote,

> "The word αρχη here, as elsewhere in Mark, does not mark a point of departure for a development in sequence, but

rather the starting point to which a given datum can be traced."[21]

By his use of such terms as "beginning", "earliest point", and "present facts" Walter Wink in his paraphrase of Marxsen tends to soften the latter's rejection of the temporal sense of αρχη. Wink "translated" Marxsen's sentence, as follows,

> "The 'beginning' is not just the point of departure for Mark's Gospel but even more the earliest point back to which present facts can be traced in order to display their meaning."[22]

The Prophecy as the Principle

My only problem with Marxsen's view is that it does not specify exactly what the "guiding principle" (αρχη) was and how it operated in Mark's argument. Before we attempt to correct this omission, it may help to discuss the translation of this key term. In the English language we express the logical sense of αρχη with the Latin derived word "principle". "Beginning" has too much of a chronological connotation to be used here. If we had used the Greek term instead, the title of William James' *Principles of Psychology* would have been called the Archai of Psychology. The Greek term is found in such words as archaeology, and archaic etc. There are several ways to express the logical sense of the Greek word αρχη: first principle, governing principle, guiding principle, organizing principle, fundamental notion or basic teaching etc. Even beginning or starting point are acceptable if they are taken in the logical sense.

It may even be significant that αρχη in Mark is singular, "guiding principle" and not plural, "basic principles." This leads us to look for a particular principle, which we find in the messenger prophecy. Therefore the first consequence of taking αρχη in the logical sense is to shift the beginning or starting point of the gospel from the activity of John the Baptist to the messenger prophecy, which can then be understood as the "guiding principle" of the gospel of Jesus Christ, Son of God.

By far the most important discussion of αρχη in Mark 1:1 is that of Allen Wikgren, one of the former editors of *The Greek New Testament*. After listing six different views of the first verse of Mark and discussing them briefly, he opted for considering the verse the title of the gospel of Mark. Then he called attention to the ambiguity of the current translation of the first word of Mark as "beginning," and suggested that an alternate translation might be more accurate.

After correctly translating αρχη as "first thing," without explanation he shifted from the singular to the plural. He claimed,

> . . . that αρχη in the Marcan passage may mean 'first thing' in the sense of 'rudiments' or 'elements' or 'essentials' of the gospel.[23]

This is the closest Wikgren comes to actually translating the "title" of Mark. If he had consistently translated αρχη as a singular, he might have found his "first thing" (principle) in the messenger prophecy. In his discussion of the parallels in Hebrews 5:12 and 6:1 he adhered to the singular in his (Goodspeed's) translation of αρχη: Heb. 5:12, "the very elements of Christian truth," and Heb. 6:1, "leaving elementary Christian teaching."[24] Of course the use of the term "Christian" is an anachronism because neither Hebrews nor Mark contain the word Christian.

If these parallels in Hebrews indicate that its author was acquainted with Mark, then he probably considered Mark the elementary instruction and his own work the more advanced teaching. Wikgren appeared to have endorsed such a view.[25] However, that was not Mark's view of his own work because his gospel contains both levels of meaning: the parable for outsiders and the interpretation for insiders.

When Wikgren objected to supplying the verb "to be" (ην) in order to connect αρχη with the messenger prophecy, he may have inadvertently involved himself in a contradiction. He claimed that one could reasonably expect a scribe to have supplied the verb "to be" if it were implied, and none did. On the other hand in regard to Mark 13: 8 he wrote,

> Αρχη των ωδινων ταυτα is a statement with a subject and a predicate in which it is imperative that the verb be supplied.[26]

How much more it would have been incumbent upon a scribe to have added the verb "to be" in this case, and yet Wikgren did not even bother to inquire as to whether one did. His assumption that the verb "to be" should be placed before the introduction to the prophecy rather than after it is problematic. Finally, his hypothetical expectation that

> ... some scribe would yield to the insistent call for an inferential particle in verse 4. 'The beginning of the gospel... (was) as was prophesied ..., (for) John came, etc.'[27]

was a direct consequence of Wikgren and *The Greek New Testament's* placement of a comma instead of a period after the prophecy.

The Principle as the Premise

Aristotle considered these αρχαι (principles), which were drawn from the opinions of great thinkers, past and present, as premises from which he could form syllogisms and by means of which he could construct a deductive science in order to make the subject in question intelligible. If we are to believe the masterful study of Aristotle by John Herman Randall Jr. making the world intelligible was what Aristotle's science was all about.[28]

In my book *Mark A Twice-Told Tale* I pointed out that

Mark called the Forerunner and Messiah John and Jesus in the first half of the gospel and Elijah and the Son of Man in the second half. I compared this to the parable and its interpretation.[29] By observing certain rhetorical conventions adopted by Mark we may be able to be more specific about the origin of this pattern, and even shed light on the elusive search for that holy grail of Markan research, its genre.

If our translation of αρχη is correct, the gospel of Mark can be read as a syllogism writ large, in which the guiding principle contained in the messenger prophecy becomes its major premise. This syllogism, which formed the backbone of the gospel's structure, can be displayed graphically as follows:

> Major Premise: God sent his messenger to prepare the way of the Lord in the desert.
> Minor Premise: John prepared the way of Jesus in the desert.
> Conclusion: Therefore, John was the messenger and Jesus is the Lord.

The major premise is identical with Mark's introduction (Mk. 1: 1-3). The elaboration of the minor premise comprises the first half of the gospel (Mk. 1: 4 – 8: 31). Since the minor premise cannot contain the conclusion, which identified John and Jesus as Elijah and the Son of Man, all Mark can do at this point is describe their respective activities and imply that they conform to the prophecy especially with regard to the order in which they appeared: John first and Jesus second. This view has obvious implications for the "secrecy" theme in Mark.

It was only in the middle of the gospel that Mark drew the conclusion which identified John as Elijah and Jesus as the Son of Man. Even here he did not do so explicitly, but rather by referring his auditors back to the messenger prophecy, "as it is written of him" and "how is it written". When Mark elaborated the conclusion of the syllogism in the second half of the gospel, he linked the death of John the Baptist, which he had described previously, with that of the Son of Man. The conclusion included Jesus predictions of his death and resurrection "on the way".

Finally, in another tightly reasoned enthymeme, Mark's Jesus identified the Messiah as David's Lord and not his son (Mk. 12: 35-37). In her book *Sowing the Gospel*, Mary Ann Tolbert discussed the above enthymeme and others.[30] An enthymeme is a shortened form of a syllogism used in public speaking in which the speaker omitted the premises that he shared with the audience, usually culturally conditioned and deeply held beliefs. In order to bring to light these hidden premises Tolbert exhibited the full syllogistic form of Mark's / Jesus' argument. In an appendix to my book I discussed at length the enthymeme about the Davidic descent of the Messiah.[31]

αρχη Elsewhere in Mark

It is worthwhile to ask whether Mark used the term αρχη elsewhere in the gospel in the logical sense. He used αρχη three other times: Mk. 10: 6, and 13: 8 and 9. In the last two references the temporal element *may* predominate: The second reference (Mk. 13: 8) referred to the beginning of the tribulation period and the third one (Mk. 13: 9) to the time since the beginning of creation.

However, in the first reference (Mk. 10: 6) the context would suggest that a non-temporal or logical meaning was primarily intended. In a complex argument about divorce Mark had Jesus appeal to God's creation as the basis of his reasoning. The poetic version in Genesis is frequently used in the marriage ceremony, but Mark's Jesus used it in a reasoned argument about the permissibility of divorce. The Pharisees had just challenged Jesus with the question as to whether it were lawful for a man to put away (divorce) his wife. Jesus in turn asked them what Moses *commanded*. They replied that Moses *permitted* divorce by a bill of divorcement. Jesus then argued that Moses *allowed* divorce because of the hardness of their hearts, but maintained that the original intention of creation was otherwise.

In order to follow Jesus' reasoning one must have both creation stories in mind. We will list them in the Genesis order although the first one is probably later than the second one.

The First Creation Story

> So God created humankind in his
> image
> in the image of God he created
> them;
> male and female he created
> them. (Gen. 1: 27)

The Second Creation Story

> —then the Lord God formed man from the dust of the ground,
> and breathed into his nostrils the breath of life;
> and the man became a living being. (Gen. 2: 7).

> So the Lord God caused a deep sleep to fall upon the man, and he slept; then he took one of his ribs and closed up its place with flesh. And the rib that the Lord God had taken from the man He made into a woman and brought her to the man. Then the man said,
> 'This at last is bone of my bones
> and flesh of my flesh;
> This one shall be called woman,
> For out of man this one was taken.'
> Therefore (Mark has 'for this reason')
> a man leaves his father and his
> mother and clings to his wife,
> and they become one
> flesh. (Gen. 2: 21-23)

After pointing out that Moses' bill of divorcement was a concession to man's weakness, Jesus continued,

Mark / Jesus' Creation Story

> But from the beginning (αρχη) of creation, 'God made them male and female.' (from the first creation story, Gen. 1: 27).
>
> For this reason a man shall leave his father and mother and be joined to his wife, and the two shall become one flesh. So they are no longer two, but one flesh. (from the second creation story, Gen. 2: 24-25).
>
> Therefore what God has joined together, let no one separate. (Mk. 10: 6-9)

Jesus' argument required the use of both creation stories. In the gospel of Mark Jesus maintained that divorce was forbidden because God joined male and female together, which required that they be created separately in the first place as in the first creation story. Just the opposite happened in the second creation story in which male and female were originally together in Adam, and God separated them by taking Adam's rib and creating woman. In the second creation story it was unnecessary for God to join man and woman together. The man simply leaves his parents and clings to his wife, and they become one flesh because they were originally created as one. The phrase "For this reason" makes more sense in the second creation story in which the rationale for a man's leaving his father and mother and clinging to his wife is that the man and woman were created together in the first place. When Mark / Jesus made this phrase follow the first creation story in which God created male and female separately at the beginning, it loses some of its force.

Mark / Jesus required the separate creation of man and woman, because his argument required that God join them together. His reasoning can be cast in the form of a syllogism.

Major Premise: What God joined together man must not separate.
Minor Premise: God joined man and wife together as one flesh.
Conclusion: Therefore, no man shall separate them.

αρχη in the Book of Hebrews

Since the view of Mark as a persuasive discourse brings that gospel closer to Hebrews, the other theological essay, sermon, or to use the author's own term, a word of exhortation, it should not be surprising to find parallels in that work to Mark's use of αρχη to mean principle. Hebrews was already considered a reasoned discourse as opposed to a story, so the chronological meaning of αρχη, beginning, was not even considered. Hagner translated Hebrews 6:1 as "The 'elementary teachings (sic) about Christ'", or "Literally, the 'beginning of the word of Christ' . . ." However, "beginning" is not the literal meaning of αρχη, but simply an alternate meaning of the word.[32] We now have a book that discusses the relationship between the story and persuasive discourse in the book of Hebrews. In his book *Understanding the Book of Hebrews* Kenneth Schenck writes about *The Story Behind The Sermon*, the subtitle of his work. In it he lumped the gospels together and compared them to Hebrews.

> "Thus while a Gospel is a 'story-as-discoursed' in a narrative, Paul's letters and Hebrews are 'stories-as-discoursed' in rhetoric."[33]

He apparently still considered the gospels as primarily narratives or stories.

The parallels to Mark 1:1 found in Hebrews 5:12 and 6:1 have not gone unnoticed.[34] They are clearer in Greek.

> Αρχη του ευαγγελιου ’Ιησου Χριστου [υιου Θεου].
> The guiding principle of the gospel of Jesus Christ, the Son of God. (Mk. 1:1).

τα στοιχεια της αρχης των λογιων του θεου.
The basic elements of the oracles of God. (Heb. 5:12)

... τον της αρχης του Χριστου λογον ...
... the basic teaching about Christ ... (Heb. 6:1)

Is it possible that the author of Hebrews is here alluding to the first verse of Mark? Notice that the singular of αρχη is used in all three quotations.

Mark portrayed Jesus' disciples as lacking understanding; the author of Hebrews chided his addressees for being dull of understanding (Heb. 5:1). He said they ought to be teachers, but instead need to be taught "The basic elements (τα στοιχεια της αρχης) of the oracles of God." (Heb. 5:12). They should be on a meat diet, but, as babes in Christ, they are still on a milk diet. Then, astonishingly, the writer of Hebrews urged his readers / hearers to leave the basic teaching about Christ and go on to perfection. The teaching that the author of Hebrews urged his readers / auditors to abandon on their journey to perfection comprised the common "Christian" teachings: repentance from dead works, faith toward God, baptisms, laying on of hands, resurrection from the dead and eternal judgment, which are also found in the gospel of Mark.

In the introduction to Hebrews (Heb. 1: 1-5) there are other parallels to the parable of the Vineyard in Mark (Mk. 12: 1-12). Again, agreement may have been mediated through a common tradition. Both Hebrews and the parable have

1. a succession of prophets through whom God spoke in the past,
2. a revelation in the last days,
3. through God's Son,
4. who is the heir, and
5. both refer to Psalm 2:7 near the beginning of their discourse.

At a minimum I would like to suggest that Hebrews looked back to a work or works like Mark, as the foundation of the gospel, a work comprised of basic or elementary teachings. The author of Hebrews not only urged his addressees to forsake these elementary teachings, but also claimed that to return to them was to crucify the Son of God again (Heb. 6:6).

The more advanced teachings were, of course, those found in his own work, which taught that Jesus was the Son of God and a High Priest after the order of Melchezedek, who offered himself as a perfect sacrifice replacing the repeated sacrifices of the "Old Testament". The author of Hebrews even claimed that once a person had become enlightened and fell away, he could not be restored through repentance, the essential part of the "elementary" teaching mentioned above. The one time repentance advocated by Hebrews corresponded to the once and for all sacrifice of Jesus. To allow a second repentance after lapsing would be to teach multiple sacrifices like those under the law, except that the sacrifice in this case would be the sacrifice or crucifixion of the Son of God again, which would be to deny that Jesus once for all sacrifice was sufficient.

We have found parallels between the content of Hebrews' introduction (Heb. 1: 1-5), and the Parable of the Vineyard (Mk. 12: 1-12). As for the form and function of Hebrews' introduction, it constituted the prooemium or rhetorical introduction to the following persuasive discourse.[35] In this role, that is, as regards its form, it is parallel to Mark 1: 1-3, the prooemium of the gospel of Mark.

Conclusion

For almost two thousand years the gospels have been taken to be primarily stories. According to John Drury, this trait accounts for their tremendous hold on our imagination:

> Stories (to use a term which deliberately begs the question of fact or fiction) communicate doctrines to the ordinary man more vividly than abstract schemes or moral advice because they are more concrete and more fun.[36]

We find it much easier to locate ourselves in the stories than to determine the points made by them in their original setting. Therefore, we strip away the argumentative framework of the stories and use them as mirrors to reflect our own concerns.

When I wrote my book *Mark A Twice-Told Tale*, I was under the influence of William Beardslee's contrast between Aristotle's poetics and rhetoric. Following Beardslee's advice I used Aristotle's poetics in combination with modern literary criticism to study Mark. Since Mark contains stories and an overriding plot, it is still valid to study the gospel of Mark in this way. Actually, the materials in Mark are suggestive of two different genres: On the one hand we have narratives or stories and on the other hand preaching or a persuasive discourse, just as light may be viewed as waves or particles. However, it is doubtful that the narrative is primary in Mark because it has not been able to accommodate the argumentative and persuasive elements in the gospel. Nor has it led to a determination of the gospel's genre.

On the other hand when we begin with the persuasive elements in Mark, rhetorical analysis can easily accommodate the story elements. It will be seen that Mark began with a conventional prooemium or introduction whose points are illustrated and elaborated in the narrative that followed. The frequent practice of scholars, such as James Robinson, of interpreting Mark through the lens of a single passage is based on a correct intuition. In my book *Mark A Twice-Told Tale*, I demonstrated a connection between the messenger prophecy and the rest of the gospel. However, I then viewed the messenger prophecy as a passion prophecy.[37] It is now clear to me that it is much more than that. Like preachers today Mark chose a text, the messenger prophecy, that generated the structure of his persuasive discourse.

Endnotes

1   Albert Schweitzer, *The Mystery of the Kingdom of God*, (New York: The Macmillan Company, 1957), p. 83.

2   Faierstein, Morris M. "Why Do the Scribes Say That Elijah Comes First?" JBL 100 (1981) 75-86.
    Allison, Dale C. "Elijah Must Come First," JBL 103 (1984) 256-58.
    Fitzmyer, Joseph A. "More About Elijah Coming First," JBL 104 (1985) 295-96.

3   St. Justin Martyr, *Dialogue With Trypho*, Tr. By Thomas B. Falls, Revised and with a New Introduction by Thomas P. Halton, Ed. By Michael Slusser, (Washington D.C.: The Catholic Univ. Press of America, 2003), p. 76.

4   *Ibid.*, p. 74.

5   *Ibid.*, p. 75.

6   Caurie Beaver, *Mark A Twice-Told Tale* (Xlibris Corporation, 2004), pp. 75-79.

7   Elaine Pagels, *Beyond Belief* (New York: Vintage Books, A Division of Random House Inc., 2003), p. 26.

8   Daryl D. Schmidt, *The Gospel of Mark*, The Scholars Bible (Sonoma, California, Polebridge Press, 1990), p. 43.

9   A.E.J. Rawlinson, *St. Mark* (London: Methuen & Co. LTD. 36 Essex Street W.C.), p. 6.

10 R.H. Lightfoot, *The Gospel Message of St. Mark* (Eugene, Oregon: Wipf & Stock Publishers, 1950), p. 15. James M. Robinson, *The Problem of History in Mark and Other Essays* Philadelphia: Fortress Press, 1982), p. 70, Note 1.

11 M. Eugene Boring, "Mk. 1: 1-15 And the Beginning of the Gospel" *Semeia 52 How Gospels Begin* (Society of Biblical Literature, 1991), p. 55.

12 Caurie Beaver, *Mark A Twice-Told Tale*, p. 45f.

13 Caurie Beaver, *Mark A Twice-Told Tale*, p. 35f.

14 C.E.B. Cranfield, *The Gospel According to St. Mark* (Cambridge: Cambridge University Press, 1959), p. 34.

15 Robert A. Guelich, *Mark 1-8: 26* Word Biblical Commentary, Vol. 34A, (Dallas, Texas Word Book Publishers, 1989), p. 6.

16 Nigel Turner, *Grammatical Insights into the New Testament* (New York: T & T Clark International A Continuum imprint, 2004), pp. 27-28.

17 John R. Donahue, S.J., and Daniel J. Harrington, S.J., *The Gospel of Mark, Sacra Pagina Series, v. 2* (Collegeville, Minnesota: A Michael Glazier Book, The Liturgical Press, 2002), pp. 59-60.

18 Ernest Best, Mark *The Gospel As Story* (Edinburgh T & T Clark 59 George Street, 1983, Reprinted 1988), p. 38.

19 Mark Horne, *The Victory According to Mark* (Moscow, ID: Canon Press, 2003), p. 43.

20 Willi Marxsen, *Mark the Evangelist*, Translated by James Boyce, Donald Juel, and William Poehlmann (Nashville: Abingdon Press, 1969), p. 42.

21 *Ibid.*

22 Walter Wink, *John the Baptist in the Gospel Tradition* (Eugene, OR.: Wipf and Stock Publishers, 2000, p. 5.

23 Allen Wikgren, "ΑΡΧΗ ΤΟΥ ΕΥΑΓΓΕΛΙΟΥ" *Journal of Biblical Literature*, 61 (1942), 17.

24 *Ibid.* p. 18.

25 *Ibid.* p. 19.

26 *Ibid.* p. 13.

27 *Ibid.* p. 13.

28 John Herman Randall Jr., *Aristotle* (New York: Columbia University Press, 1960), pp. 32f.

29 Caurie Beaver, *Mark A Twice-Told Tale*, pp. 107f.

30 Mary Ann Tolbert, *Sowing the Gospel* (Minneapolis: Fortress Press, 1989), pp. 250-257.

31 Caurie Beaver, *Mark A Twice-Told Tale*, pp. 209-216

32 Donald A. Hagner, *Encountering the Book of Hebrews* (Grand Rapids, Michigan: Baker Academic, a division of Baker Book House Company, 2004), p. 86.

33 Kenneth Schenck, *Understanding Hebrews: The Story Behind The Sermon* (Louisville, Kentucky: Westminster John Knox Press, 2003), p. 111 n. 9.

34 C.E.B. Cranfield, *The Gospel According to Mark*, p.34.

35 Victor C. Pfitzner, *Hebrews* (Nashville: Abingdon Press, 1997), p. 22.

36 John Drury, *Tradition and Design in Luke's Gospel: A Study in Early Christian Historiography* (Atlanta: John Knox Press, 1977), p. 1.

37 Caurie Beaver, *Mark A Twice-Told Tale*, pp. 65-85.

AFTERWORD

In the words of Rousseau this book is about "the inventor" of the gospel story, or, at least one of them, for there were many, four of which were included in the New Testament. Rousseau could not imagine that such a story could have been invented, because he was a true child of the Enlightenment, which tended to devalue tradition and think of creativity as the product of unaided reason.

However, it was precisely the rich history of tradition that made possible a story such as the gospel of Mark. In his book The River of God, Greg Riley described the history of Christian origins as a great river whose flow was punctuated by the influx of various tributaries enriching the main stream. The focus of Riley's book was on the content of these traditions, and the hydra like shape they assumed at the beginning and end of the stream.

In my opinion a similar process occurred in connection with the forms or genres of the traditions. Like the traditions, themselves, the genre vessels in which they were carried proceeded down the tributaries and jostled one another as they entered the main stream. Concerning this process of genre formation, Frank Kermode wrote, "New genres are formed from realignments of existing genres." Already in the Torah, we have a combination of myths, legends, genealogies, king lists, and laws to form an extended epic. In these forms we see the influence of the creation and flood stories of Babylonia and the laws of Hammurabi. At various points there entered the main stream other forms such as fables, parables, psalms, proverbs, oracles, prophecies, and wisdom sayings.

The Hellenistic period, in particular, led to a veritable explosion of genres such as allegory, history, drama, and letter/epistle etc. Not one Old Testament book is in the form of a letter, but the majority of the New Testament books are in the form of a letter or epistle. This increase in letter writing may have been a function of growing literacy in the Hellenistic Roman Period. Persian dualism combined with Hellenistic periodization and Hebrew prophecy to form the gloomy apocalyptic genre. Also, the stories of the Bible were retold in Hellenistic genres: the Exodus story was turned into drama by a certain Ezekiel and the story of Moses was retold as that of a hero.

Finally, it is to Greek literature that we owe the concentration on the life of individual heroes such as Daniel in the book by that name and Jesus in the gospel of Mark. In the earlier biblical traditions the lives of Adam, Noah, Joseph, and Moses were subordinated to the overarching epic in which they were embedded. In Philo of Alexandria's Life of Moses, the story of the lawgiver was retold in Hellenistic biographical form. Moses was described as a divine/human savior god not unlike Jesus the Son of God in Mark

We are not here confronted with modern biography or story telling, which finds meaning in the interaction and psychological development of the various characters. In such realistic narrative a story can mean what it says. This was seldom true of ancient storytelling in which meaning resided in the interaction of the various characters with the ideal or divine realm. The story usually had a deeper meaning which served as an example by which to shape one's life. We will attempt to show how Mark was a product of the realignment of genres in the Hellenistic period.

Just as Mark was the product of various tributaries of traditions, my own work is the outcome of many modern streams of scholarship, especially German (Schweitzer, Wrede, and Marxsen etc.) and Anglo-American (Lightfoot and Robinson etc.). The author whose works assisted me most in completing this work is James M. Robinson and the author whose works helped me to understand the significance of what I have accomplished is Greg Riley. Finally, it was Gerlof D. Homan at Central State University in Oklahoma who taught me history and historical method. After reading his American Mennonites and the Great War 1914-1918, I am not surprised to find that he is not only a great teacher but a great historian as well.

Furthermore, I would like to acknowledge Dr. James M. Robinson's great care in proofreading the manuscript and for his gracious comments that went beyond anything I could have anticipated. I would also like to thank two librarians at the School of Theology at Claremont, Elaine Walker and Betty Clements for their generous help in acquiring research materials. A final word of thanks is due to my wife, Sandra, whose labor under very difficult circumstances, has made this work presentable. No work is perfect. All are ultimately the product of the stream of scholarship which can only be augmented by the individual by a process that Frank Kermode called "divination", which, itself, upon reconsideration is found to reflect latent tendencies in the scholarly tradition.

ENDNOTES

1. John Drury, *Critics of the Bible* 1724-1873, Cambridge University Press, 1989, pp. 19-20.
2. John Drury, *Critics of the Bible* 1724-1873, p. 1.
3. James M. Robinson, "Nineteenth Century Theology as Heritage and Fate," *The Drew Gateway*. Vol. 44, 1974, p.69.
4. John Drury, *Critics of the Bible* 1724-1873, p. 3.
5. John Drury, *Critics of the Bible* 1724-1873, p. 9.
6. Alfred Edersheim, *The Life and Times of Jesus the Messiah* 8th Ed. rev. New York: Longman's Green & Co. 1915, p. xiii
7. Norman Perrin, *Rediscovering the Teaching of Jesus*, New York and Evanston: Harper & Row Publishers, 1967, p.39.
8. Albert Schweitzer, *The Quest of the Historical Jesus*, New York: The Macmillan Co., 1957, pp 358-360.
9. Albert Schweitzer, *Out of My Life and Thought*, Tr. By C. T. Campion, New York: 1933, p. 119.
10. Here belong such works as Frank Kermode's *Genesis of Secrecy*, David Rhoads' and Donald Michie's *Mark As Story*, and Norman R. Peterson's *Literary Criticism for New Testament Critics*.
11. Albert Schweitzer, *The Quest of the Historical Jesus*, p. 238
12. James M. Robinson, *A New Quest of the Historical Jesus and Other Essays*, Philadelphia: Fortress Press, 1983, p.38.
13. Sean P. Kealy, *Mark's Gospel: A History of its Interpretation*, New York/Ramsey: Paulist Press, 1982, p.1.
14. W. Ward Gasque, *A History of the Interpretation of the Acts of the Apostles*, Peabody Mass.: Hendrickson Pub;, 1975, p. 4.
15. James Blevins, *The Messianic Secret in Markan Research*, 1901-1976, Washington D.C.: University Press of America, 1981, p. 105.
16. Mary Ann Tolbert, *Sowing the Gospel*, Minneapolis: Fortress Press, 1989, pp. 25 ff.

17 See Wayne Booth's *The Rhetoric of Fiction*, and Seymour Chatman's *Story and Discourse*.
18 Frank J. Matera, *What Are They Saying About Mark?*, New York/Mahwah: Paulist Press, 1987, pp. 76 and 86.
19 Albert Schweitzer, *The Mystery of the Kingdom of God*, New York: The Macmillan Co., 1957, p.112.
20 Albert Schweitzer, *The Mystery of the Kingdom of God*, p. 104.
21 James M. Robinson, *A New Quest of the Historical Jesus and Other Essays*, Philadelphia: Fortress Press, 1983, p. 177.
22 John Drury, *The Parables in the Gospels*, New York: Crossroad Publishing Co., 1985, p. 4.
23 James M. Robinson, *The Problem of History in Mark and Other Marcan Studies*, Philadelphia: Fortress Press, 1982, p. 14.
24 Harold Riley, *The Making of Mark*, Macon, Georgia: Mercer University Press, 1989, pp. 77-78.
25 G.M. Styles, "The Priority of Mark" in C. F. D. Moule's *The Birth of the New Testament*, San Francisco: Harper and Row, 1982, p. 294.
26 Hans Conzelmann, *The Theology of Luke*, trans. By Geoffrey Buswell, New York: Harper and Row, 1960, and Bornkamm, Barth, and Held's *Tradition and Interpretation in Matthew*, trans. By Percy Scott, Philadelphia: The Westminster Press, 1963.
27 Charles W. Hedrick and Robert Hodgson Hr. Eds. *Nag Hammadi Gnosticism and Early Christianity*, Peabody Mass.: Hendrickson, 1986, pp. 127 ff.
28 John Drury, *Tradition and Design in Luke*, Atlanta: John Knox Press, 1977, p. 40.
29 Albert Schweitzer, *The Quest of the Historical Jesus*, p. 330.
30 John Drury, *Critics of the Bible.* 1724-1873.
31 Albert Schweitzer, *The Quest of the Historical Jesus*, pp. 330 ff.
32 James Blevins, *The Messianic Secret in Markan Research*, 1901-1976, Washington D.C.: University Press of America, 1981, p. 119.
33 Frederick C. Grant, *The Earliest Gospel*, New York/Nashville: Abingdon, 1943, pp. 125 ff.
34 R. H. Lightfoot, *Locality and Doctrine in the Gospels*, London: Hadderands, 1938.

35 Willi Marxsen, *Mark the Evangelist*, trans. By James Boyce, Donald Juel, William Poehlmann with Roy A. Harrisville, Nashville: Abingdon Press, 1969.
36 James M. Robinson, *The Problem of History in Mark and Other Marcan Studies*, Philadelphia: Fortress Press, 1982, pp. 40-53.
37 Hans Frei, *Eclipse of the Biblical Narrative: A Study in Eighteenth and Nineteenth Century Hermeneutics*, New Haven and London: Yale University Press, 1974, p. 217.
38 Marna Hooker, *The Message of Mark*, London: Epworth Press, 1983, p. 3.
39 William A Beardslee, *Literary Criticism of the New Testament*, Philadelphia: Fortress Press, 1970. See also Burton Mack's *Rhetoric and the New Testament*, Minneapolis: Fortress Press, 1990.
40 John Drury, *Parables in the Gospels*, New York: Crossroad, 1985, pp. 1-6.
41 Quentin Quesnell, *The Mind of Mark*, Rome: Ponitfical Biblical Institute, 1969.
42 Mary Ann Tolbert, *Perspectives On the Parables*, Philadelphia: Fortress Press, 1979, pp. 48-50.
43 Mary Ann Tolbert, *Sowing the Gospel*, pp. 2 ff.
44 James M. Robinson, *The Problem of History in Mark and Other Marcon Studies*, (Philadelphia: Fortress Press, 1982), p. 79.
45 Saint Augustine, *The City of God*, Translated by Marcs Dods, (New York: Random House, Inc., The Modern Library, 1950), p. 719.
46 Theodore J. Weeden, *Mark: Traditions in Conflict*, (Philadelphia: Fortress Press, 1971), p. 135.
47 Jeffrey Siker, *Disinheriting the Jews*, Louisville Kentucky: Westminster / John Knox Press, 1991.
48 John Drury, *The Parables in the Gospels*, New York: Crossroad Publishing Co., 1985.
49 Mary Ann Tolbert, *Sowing the Gospel*, Minneapolis: Fortress Press, 1989, pp. 231f. and 271f.
50 John Drury, *The Parables in the Gospel*, p. 66.
51 Donald Juel, *Messianic Exegesis*, Philadelphia: Fortress Press, 1988, p. 142.

52. Jack Miles, *God A Biography*, New York: Vintage Books, A Division of Random House Inc., 1966.
53. Elaine Pagels, *The Origin of Satan*, (New York: Random House Inc. Vintage Gooks, 1996), p.8.
54. Martin Hengel, *Studies in the Gospel of Mark*. Trans. By John Gowden (Philadelphia: Fortress Press, 1985), p.8. Although I agree with his analysis, it does not support his conclusion about the connection of the gospel with Peter.
55. Mary Ann Tolbert, *Sowing the Gospel*, (Minneapolis: Fortress Press, 1989), p. 252.
56. Mary Ann Tolbert, *Sowing the Gospel: Mark's World in Literary-Historical Perspective*, (Minneapolis: Fortress Press, 1989), p. 44.
57. Jack Miles, *God: A Biography*, (New York: A Division of Random House, Inc., 1995), p. 17.
58. Morna Hooker, *The Gospel According to Saint Mark* (Peabody, Massachusetts: Hendrickson Publishers, 1991), p. 306. βλέπετε could be translated "lookout!" because the verb βλέπω means "I see or look." See also Mary Ann Tolbert's *Sowing the Gospel*, p. 150.
59. Anthony Collins, *Discourse of the Grounds and Reasons of the Christian Religion*. (New York: Garland Publishing, Inc.), 1724, pp. 39f.
60. C. R. North, *The Suffering Servant in Deutero-Isaiah: An Historical and Critical Study*, (London: Geoffrey Cumberledge, Oxford University Press, 1956), p. 218.
61. Curtis Beach, *The Gospel of Mark: Its Making and Meaning*, (New York: Harper & Brothers, 1959), p. 88.
62. James G. Williams, *Gospels Against Parable: Mark's Language of Mystery*, (Almond Bible and Literature Series, 12), 1985, p.54.
63. Howard Clark Key, *Jesus in History*, (New York: Harcourt Brace Jovanovich, Inc., 1970), p. 146.
64. Sean Kealey, *Mark's Gospel: A History of its Interpretation: From the Beginning Until 1979*, (New York, Ramsey: Paulist Press, 1982), p.24.
65. Robert Alter, *The Art of Biblical Poetry*, (New York: Basic Books, Inc., Publishers, 1985), p. 19.
66. Joel Marcus, *The Way of the Lord*, (Louisville Kentucky: Westminster/John Knox Press, 1992), p. 96 and 108.

67 Vincent Taylor, *The Gospel According to St. Mark*, (Macmillan St. Martin's Press, 1966), p. 395.
68 D. E. Nineham, *The Gospel of St. Mark*, (Middlesex England: Penguin Books Ltd., 1963), p. 241.
69 Howard Clark Kee, *Jesus in History*, (New York: Harcourt Brace Jovanovich, Inc., 1970), p. 148
70 *Ibid.*, p. 146
71 *Ibid.* p. 146.
72 Morna D. Hooker, *The Gospel According to Saint Mark*, Peabody, Massachusetts: Hendrickson Publisher, 1991), p. 285.
73 Willi Marxsen, *Mark the Evangelist*, (New York: Abingdon Press, 1969), p. 37.
74 Ulrich Mauser, *Christ in the Wilderness*, (Naperville, Ill. Alec R. Allenson, Inc., 1963), p. 77f.
75 Josephus, *The Jewish War*, Translated by G. A. Williamson, Revised by E. Mary Smallwood, Penguin Books, 1981, p. 192.
76 Howard Clark Kee, *Community of the New Age:* Studies in Mark's Gospel, Philadelphia: The Westminster Press, 1977), p. 111.
77 Aloysius M. Ambrozic, *The Hidden Kingdom*, (Washington, D.C.: The Catholic Biblical Association of America, 1972), pp. 19-20.
78 Werner Kelber, *The Kingdom in Mark*, (Philadelphia: Fortress Press, 1974), p.67.
79 Werner H. Kelber, Ed., *The Passion in Mark*, (Philadelphia: Fortress Press, 1976), p. 34.
80 Stephen H. Smith, *A Lion With Wings*, p. 43. See the more detailed study of the term in David Peabody's, *Mark As Composer*, (Macon, GA: Mercer University Press, 1987), p. 115f.
81 Robert M. Fowler, *Loaves and Fishes*, (Chico, California: Scholars Press, 1981), p. 159.
82 Werner Kelber, *The Kingdom in Mark*, p. 99.
83 Marvin W. Meyers, "The Youth in the Secret Gospel of Mark," *Semeia*, No. 49, (1990), p. 147.
84 William R. Farmer, *The Synoptic Problem*, (New York: The Macmillan Co., 1964), p. 149.
85 Norman Perrin, *A Modern Pilgrimage in New Testament Christology*, (Philadelphia: Fortress Press, 1974), p. 10.

86. Anthony Collins, *A Discourse of the Grounds and Reasons of the Christian Religion*, p.39 f.
87. Judith Hermann, *Trauma and Recovery*, (New York: Basic Books, A Division of Harper Collins Publishers, 1992), p. 175.
88. Origen, *On First Principles*, Trans. by G.W. Butterworth, (Gloucester: Mass., 1973), p. 285 and 286.
89. Beryl Smalley, *The Study of the Bible in the Middle Ages*, (Indiana: University of Notre Dame Press, 1964), pp. 1-26.
90. Werner George Kümmel, *The New Testament: The History of the Investigation of Its Problems*, Tr. By S. McLeon Gilmour and Howard C. Kee, (New York: Abingdon Press, 1972), p. 22.
91. Matthew Tindal, *Christianity As Old As Creation*, (Stuttgart—Bad Connstatt, 1967), passim.
92. Thomas Paine, *The Age of Reason*, (New York: A Citadel Press Book, 1991), p. 109.
93. Thomas Woolston, *Six discourses On The Miracles of Our Saviour*, (New York & London: Garland Publishing, Inc., 1979), passim.
94. Anthony Collins, *A Discourse on the Grounds and Reasons of the Christian Religion*, passim.
95. Beryle Smalley, *The Study of the Bible in the Middle Ages*, pp. 83 ff. and pp. 112 ff.
96. David Hume, *Dialogues Concerning Natural Religion*, (Indianapolis: Bobbs-Merrill Educational Publishing, 1947), p. 45 ff.
97. Beryl Smalley, *The Study of the Bible in the Middle Ages*, p. 28.
98. Robert M. Grant and David Tracy, *A Short History of the Interpretation of the Bible*, (Philadelphia: Fortress Press, 1984), p. 59.
99. Joachim Jeremias, *The Parables of Jesus*, Tr. By S. H. Hooke, (New York: Charles Scribner's Sons, 1963), p. 11-12
100. John Drury, "The Sower, the Vineyard, and the Place of Allegory in the Interpretation of Mark's Parables," *Journal of Biblical Literature*. New Series Vol. 24, 1973, p. 368.
101. Joel Marcus, *The Mystery of the Kingdom of God*, p. 41. He described the parables as "realistic" " . . . at least according to first century methods and conceptions of agriculture."
102. Marvin W. Meyer, *Who Do People Say I Am?*, (Grand Rapids, Michigan: William B. Eerdmans Publishing Company, 1983), p. 29.

[103] John Drury, *The Parables in the Gospels*, (New York: Crossroad, 1985), p. 52.
[104] *Ibid.*, p. 52.
[105] David Rhoads and Donald Michie, *Mark As Story*, (Philadelphia: Fortress Press, 1982), p. 129.
[106] William Wrede, *The Messianic Secret*, (Cambridge and London, 1971), passim.
[107] James M. Robinson, *The Problem of History in Mark*, p. 73.
[108] Stephen H. Smith, *A Lion With Wings: A Narrative-Critical Approach to Mark's Gospel*, (Sheffield, England, Sheffield Academic Press, 1996), p. 156.
[109] Albert Schweitzer, *The Mysticism of Paul the Apostle*, (New York: The Macmillan Co., 1956), p. 236.
[110] *Ibid.*, 236-237.
[111] James M. Robinson, *The Problem of History in Mark: And Other Marcan Studies*, (Philadelphia: Fortress Press, 1982), p. 74.
[112] *Ibid.*, p. 74, note 1
[113] *Ibid.*, p. 74
[114] M. Robert Mansfield, *Spirit and Gospel in Mark*, (Peabody, Mass.: Hendrickson Publisher, Inc., 1987) p. ix.
[115] *Ibid.*, p. 25.
[116] *Ibid.*, p. 26 (See also p. 110 and p. 137).
[117] Ernest Haenchen, *The Acts of the Apostles*, (Philadelphia: The Westminster Press, 1971), p. 142.
[118] H. A. Blair, "Spirit-Baptism in St. Mark's Gospel," *Church Quarterly Review*, Vol. 155, 1954, p. 370. See G. W. H. Lampe's answer to Blair in "Spirit-Baptism or Baptism into Jesus Christ" *Church Quarterly Review*, Vol. 156, 1955, pp. 82-87.
[119] Alan Culpepper, "Mark 10:50: Why mention the Garment?" *Journal of Biblical Literature*, 1982, pp. 131-132.
[120] Jonathan Z. Smith, "Garments of Shame," *History of Religions* 5 (1966), pp. 217-238.
[121] Robin Scroggs and Kent J. Groff, "Baptism in Mark: Dying and Rising With Christ." *Journal of Biblical Literature*, Vol. 92 (1973), pp. 531-48.
[122] Rudolph Bultmann, *The History of the Synoptic Tradition*, Translated

by John Marsh, (New York: Harper and row Publishers, 1968), pp. 234-235.

[123] John Drury, *Critics of the Bible*, (New York: Cambridge University Press, 1989), p. 6.

[124] Albert Schweitzer, *The Mystery of the Kingdom of God*, (New York: The MacMillan Co., 1957) p. 103-104.

[125] G.H. Boobyer, "The Eucharistic Interpretation of the Miracle of the Loaves in St. Mark's Gospel," *Journal of Theological Studies*, Vol. 3, 1952, p. 162.

[126] Quentin Quesnell, *This Good News: An Introduction to Catholic Theology of the New Testament*, (Milwaukee: The Bruce Publishing Co., 1964), p. 172.

[127] William Wrede, *The Messianic Secret*, Tr. By J.C.G. Greig, (Cambridge and London: James Clarke & Co. Ltd., 1971), p. 207.

[128] D.E. Nineham, *Saint Mark* (In the Pelican New Testament Commentaries, Penguin Books, 1963), p. 211. See also Alan Richardson's, *The Miracle-Stories of the Gospels*, (London: SCM Press Ltd., 1941), pp. 94 ff.

[129] Robert Fowler, *Loaves and Fishes*, (Scholars Press, Society of Biblical Literature Dissertation Series, 1981), p. 60.

[130] *Ibid*, p. 60.

[131] *Ibid*, p. 110.

[132] *Ibid*, p. 86.

[133] D. E. Nineham, *Saint Mark*, p. 179. See also Howard Clark Kee's *Community of the New Age*, (Philadelphia: The Westminster Press, 1977), p. 111.

[134] Austin Farrer, *A Study of Mark*, (Jacre Press Westminster, 1951), pp. 290 ff.

[135] John Drury, "Mark," *The Literary Guide to the Bible*, Eds. Robert Alter and Frank Kermode, (Cambridge, Mass., Harvard University Press, 1987), p. 414.

[136] *Ibid.*, p. 415. See also Quentin Quesnell's *The Good News*, p. 172, and Austin Farrer, *A Study in St. Mark*, p. 303.

[137] James G. Williams, *Gospel Against Parable: Mark's Language of Mystery*, (Almond, JSOT Press, 1985), p. 133.

138. Quentin Quesnell, *The Mind of Mark*, (Rome: Pontifical Biblical Institute, 1969), p. 40.
139. D.E. Nineham, *Saint Mark*, p. 199.
140. Aristotle, *The Rhetoric and Poetics*, Trans by W. Rhys Roberts and Ingram Bywater, (New York: The Modern Library, Random House Inc., 1954), pp. 236-237. See also Gilbert G. Bilzikian, *The Liberated Gospel*, (Grand rapids, Michigan: Baker Book House, 1977), p.100, and Curtis Beach, *The Gospel of Mark* (New York: Harper & Brothers, 1959), p. 46.
141. Norman Perrin, *The New Testament An Introduction*, (New York: Harcourt Brace Jovanovich, Inc., 1974), p. 155-6.
142. Shirley Jackson Case, *The Evolution of Early Christianity*, (Chicago: The University of Chicago Press, 1914), p. 230. David R. Cartlidge and David L. Dungan, *Documents for the Study of the Gospels*, (Philadelphia: fortress Press, 1980), p. 14. See also John J. Collins' discussion of messianism in the Dead Sea Scrolls in James H. Charlesworth & Walter P. Weaver, editors, *The Dead Sea Scrolls and the Christian Faith* (Harrisburg, Pa.: Trinity Press International, 1998), p. 20 ff.
143. Aristotle, *The Rhetoric and the Poetics*, p. 237.
144. Christopher Bryan *A Preface to Mark*, (New York: Oxford University Press, 1993), pp. 173-4.
145. Adela Yarbro Collins, *The Beginning of the Gospel: Probings of Mark in Context*, (Minneapolis: Fortress Press), p. 145-6.
146. Seymour Chatman, *Story and Discourse*.
147. Pheme Perkins, *The Gnostic Dialogue: The Early Church and the Crisis of Gnosticism*, (New York: Paulist Press, 1980), pp. 37 f.
148. Adela Yarbro Collins, *The Beginnings of the Gospel*, p. 146, 7.
149. Edgar Hennecke and Wilhelm Schneemelcher, *The New Testament Apocrypha Vol. I*, Translated by Mc L. Wilson, (Philadelphia: The Westminster Press, 1963), p. 186.
150. C.F.Evans, *Resurrection and the New Testament*, (Naperville, Ill.: Alec R. Allenson Inc., 1970), p. 65.
151. Daryl D. Schmidt, *The Gospel of Mark*, The scholars Bible version (Sonoma, Ca.: Polebridge Press, 1990), pp. 153-155.

[152] Mark Allan Powell, *God With Us: A Pastoral Theology of Matthew's Gospel*, (Minneapolis: Fortress Press, 1995), passim.

[153] Alan Culpepper, *Anatomy of the Fourth Gospel*, (Philadelphia: Fortress Press, 1983), p.p. 9-11.

[154] Shaye J. D. Cohen, *From the Maccabees to the Mishnah*, Philadelphia: The Westminster Press, 1987), p. 206.

[155] Frank McConnell, ed, *The Bible and the Narrative Tradition* (New York/Oxford: Oxford University Press, 1986), p. 113.

[156] See Oscar Cullman's chapter on "The plurality of the Gospels as a Theological Problem in Antiquity" in his *The Early Church: Studies in Early Christian History and Theology*. Edited by A.J.B. Higgins (The Westminster Press: Philadelphia, 1966), p.p. 39-54.

[157] See discussion by Henri-Charles Puech in Edgar Hennecke, Wilhelm Scneemelcher, *New Testament Apocrypha*, Translated by R. McL. Wilson, (Wesminister Press: Philadelphia, 1963), Vol. I, p. 272.

[158] Ibid., Vol. I, p. 43.

[159] William Wrede, *The Messianic Secret*, Translated by J.C.G. Greig, (James Clark and Co. LTD: Cambridge and London, 1971).P.186.

[160] James M. Robinson, General Editor, *The Nag Hammadi Library*. "The Apocalypse of Peter," Translated by Roger A. Bullard, (Harper and Row Publishers: San Francisco, 1977), p. 344.

[161] E Hennecke and W. Schneemelcher, *New Testament Apocrypha*, Vol. I, p. 186.

[162] Rudolf Bultmann, *Primitive Christianity in its Contemporary Setting*, (New York: Meridian Books, 1956), p. 71.

[163] J. Andrew Overman, *Matthew's Gospel; and Formative Judaism*, (Minneapolis: Fortress Press, 1990).

[164] Norman Perrin, *The New Testament An Introduction*, (Chicago: Harcourt Brace Javanovich Inc., 1974), p. 136.

[*] My friend's name is Spencer Crump. He is an inspiring and perhaps too generous critic.

[165] John Knox, *Chapters in a Life of Paul*, (Macon, Ga.: Mercer University Press, 1987), p. ix.

[166] Norman Perrin, *The New Testament an Introduction*, p. 90.

167 Martin Hengel, *Judaism and Hellenism*, (Philadelphia: Fortress Press, 1974).
168 Norman Perrin, *The New Testament An Introduction*, p. 40.
169 Elaine Pages, *The Origin of Satan*, (New York: Vintage Books, A Division of Random House Inc., 1996), p.82.
170 Harvie Branscomb, *The Gospel of Mark*, The Moffatt New Testament Commentary, (London: Hodder Stoughton Limited, 1952), p. 222.
171 *Ibid.*, p. 222.
172 *Ibid.*, p. 222.
173 *Ibid.*, p.222.
174 Hugh Anderson, *The Gospel of Mark*, New Century Bible Commentary, (Grand Rapids: Wm. B. Eerdmans Publ. Co., 1976), p. 284.
175 *Ibid.*, p. 284.
176 *Ibid.*, p. 284.
177 Eduard Schweizer, *The Good News According to Mark*, (Richmond, Virginia: John Knox Press, 1970), p. 256.
178 *Ibid.*, p. 256.
179 Mary Ann Tolbert, *Sowing the Gospel*, (Minneapolis: Fortress Press, 1989), pp. 255-6.
180 *Ibid.*, p. 256.
181 *Ibid.*, p. 126.
182 *Ibid.*, p. 251.
183 *Ibid.*, p. 252
184 Werner Kelber, *The Kingdom in Mark*, (Philadelphia: Fortress Press, 1974), pp. 95-97.
185 James C. Vanderkam, *The Dead Sea Scrolls Today*, (Grand Rapids, Michigan: William B. Eerdmans Publishing Company, 1994), p. 177.

www.ingramcontent.com/pod-product-compliance
Lightning Source LLC
Chambersburg PA
CBHW051634230426
43669CB00013B/2298